The Decision to Parent:
A TEACHING GUIDE

EDITED BY **JERELYN B. SCHULTZ**

WITH **PENNY RALSTON, BARBARA ROUGVIE, MARGARET JAN KELLY**

THE IOWA STATE UNIVERSITY PRESS / AMES

Printed by
The Iowa State University Press
Ames, Iowa 50010

First edition, 1980

International Standard Book Number: 0-8138-1595-9

ACKNOWLEDGEMENTS

The teaching guide on The Decision to Parent resulted because home economics educators at various professional levels were concerned about the rise in teenage pregnancy and parenthood. They contributed resources so that educational materials could be developed which might motivate teenagers to postpone parenthood until they are ready for these experiences.

The effort was facilitated financially and administratively by the Career Education Division of the Iowa Department of Public Instruction and the Home Economics Education Department at Iowa State University. Appreciation is expressed to Gladys Grabe and Mavis Kelley from the Iowa Department of Public Instruction for their foresight and support of the curriculum development effort. Special thanks goes to Dr. Ruth P. Hughes, Head of the Home Economics Education Department, for her encouragement through allocation of responsibilities and resources to facilitate the research and development efforts which resulted in the present form of the guide.

Appreciation is expressed to the individuals who served as members of the Parent Education Task Force: Elizabeth Alden from the University of Iowa, Helen Burris from the University of Northern Iowa, Carole Gilliam from March of Dimes, Bette Samuels from Des Moines Area Community College, Shean Sherzan from the Iowa Council for Children, Suzanne Sievers from Jefferson High School, Jan Winslow from Indian Hills Community College, and Gretchen Woeste from the Des Moines Independent Community School District. Their advice throughout the course of the effort was valued highly.

Six Iowa home economics teachers deserve special recognition. Their participation in curriculum development workshops resulted in the working draft of the curricular materials. They were Elizabeth Cook of Des Moines,

Nancy Gesy of Denison, Caye Keith of Sioux City, Marsha Molis of Davenport, Bonnie Rohlena of Van Horne, and Judith Wilson of Irwin. Their contributions were vital to the success of the project.

Two faculty members in the College of Home Economics were generous with their time and talent. They served as subject-matter and education consultants in various capacities during the development of the curricular materials: Margaret Torrie from Home Economics Education and Nancy Meredith from Family Environment. Appreciation also is expressed to other faculty members in the Department of Home Economics Education for their interest, encouragement, and professional expertise.

The last group to be cited for their cooperation are the seven Iowa home economics teachers who implemented the curricular materials in their classes. They were: Ruth Buck of Newton, Mary Cannon of Tipton, Sandy Kristensen of Audubon, Mary Ann Jackson of Cedar Rapids, Mary Preston of Waterloo, Sharon Sibert of Des Moines, and Betty Yungschlager of Griswold. Their comments and suggestions were valued highly and improved the final curricular materials.

CONTENTS

INTRODUCTION

Adolescent pregnancy has emerged as an important social problem in America today. Despite a fall in birthrates for the population at large, the number of illegitimate conceptions among teenage girls has increased dramatically. Adolescents bore one-fifth of the nation's children in 1978, and a large proportion planned to keep and raise their children themselves. In many cases school-age parents are not physically, psychologically, emotionally, or economically ready to assume the responsibilities of parenthood. This has led to concern over the quality of care children of school-age parents will receive.

One means available to help assure that the care needs of these children are met is to prepare young people for the responsibilities of parenthood. For all practical purposes the secondary schools present the last universal opportunity for parenthood education. Parenthood education should provide teenagers with a knowledge base upon which to make decisions regarding the assumption of parenthood, and if and when applicable, the knowledge and skills to perform parental responsibilities effectively. In 1976 Congress enacted Public Law 94-482 mandating the inclusion of family living, parenthood education, and child development and guidance in vocational consumer and homemaking programs.

Parenthood education provides the information needed by potential and actual parents to develop the knowledge, skills, and attitudes essential for making quality decisions about the assumption of the parental role and, if and when assumed, effective role performance. Child development and parenthood education are not synonymous. Child development emphasizes growth and development of children, while parenthood education stresses how to parent developing children.

Effective parenthood education programs should meet the parenting needs of the students they serve. The parenting needs of secondary students were assessed by a 50-item Parenting Information Inventory in 1978 as a basis for planning parenthood education programs. Students expressed the greatest need for information on planning and decision making, adolescent social development, and parenting and child care. They also indicated a need for information on teenage pregnancy, sex education, love and marriage, basic nutrition, current societal trends in family life, and special responsibilities of teenagers. These needs were combined into three major topics for a parenthood education curriculum:

The Decision to Parent

Sexuality and the Adolescent

Caring for Children in Today's Society

The highest priority needs expressed by students were for information related to goal setting and attainment, responsibilities for planning their own lives, and decision making. Therefore, the first topic developed into a curriculum module was The Decision to Parent.

A group of six home economics teachers reviewed the competencies, subcompetencies, and generalizations. They suggested learning activities that could be used in teaching the information to secondary students. The resulting materials were field tested and refined.

Modules will be developed for the other two topics, Sexuality and the Adolescent and Caring for Children in Today's Society, during the next several years. The module on Sexuality and the Adolescent will address identity development during adolescence, the influence of interpersonal relationships on sexual attitudes and behaviors, and pregnancy and birth. The third module will be concerned with raising children in contemporary society. It will include parenting developing children, single parent families, child abuse, and other issues affecting children and families today. The three modules will represent a parenthood education curriculum designed to meet the needs of teenagers.

It is hoped as a result of these materials students will be better able to make decisions regarding the assumption of parental responsibilities and will be motivated to postpone parenthood until they are ready for these experiences. Participation in the learning activities in this module and the succeeding modules does not guarantee that students will make quality decisions regarding parenthood; however, they will have a greater appreciation of the factors involved and the skills needed to be an effective parent.

DEFINITIONS

MAJOR COMPETENCY: The knowledge, skills and judgments the learners will demonstrate at the end of the instructional program. In essence, major competencies are program goals.

SUBCOMPETENCY: The type of behavior the learner is expected to exhibit as a result of participation in the learning activities and conclusion of generalizations.

GENERALIZATION: Statements that express an underlying truth, have an element of universality, and usually indicate relationships between concepts.

LEARNING ACTIVITIES: Opportunities provided for the learners to interact with the content under consideration. The two components of a learning activity are content and teaching technique.

RESOURCES: All instructional materials, print and nonprint, needed to carry out suggested learning activities.

MODULE ORGANIZATION

Resources contained in this module, The Decision to Parent, are directed toward the development of the two major competencies:

> The student can appraise the variety of responsibilities involved in being a parent
>
> and
>
> The student can utilize the decision-making process in determining if and when to become a parent.

The major competencies should be presented in the order stated above because the first major competency builds the cognitive understanding of parenthood necessary for students to make the decisions referred to in the second major competency.

Included for each major competency are supporting subcompetencies, generalizations, learning activities, and resources for the students and teacher. The module is organized into three sections: the teaching/learning component, the appendices, and the bibliography. Gray dividing pages are used to identify the beginning of each of these sections.

A double page, four column format is used for the teacher/learning component. Columns are read from left to right and are labeled subcompetencies, possible generalizations, learning activities, and resources. The major competency being developed is stated across the top of the page on the left. In the teaching/learning section, a small

placed in the upper right corner above the resources column indicates a new subcompetency is being introduced.

Individual learning activities listed in the third column are numbered. The first number at the left of each learning activity identifies the generalization to which it corresponds. Following the decimal point is the number of the learning activity associated with the generalization. For example, 2.3 written before a learning activity indicates that it is the third activity developed for generalization two. When two numbers separated by a dash (1.0-5.0) are found to the left of a learning activity, the learning activity will contribute to all generalizations one through five.

In some instances a small symbol appears in the margin at the left of a learning activity. The four symbols used and the significance of each are:

- □ - the activity may be suitable for an FHA project.
- ■ - the activity may be appropriate for a mainstreamed class.
- ○ - the activity may be adaptable for junior high.
- ● - the activity may involve sensitive areas. Evaluate class and community carefully before using.

A variety of learning activities and resources are suggested so that a teacher may select those most applicable to the needs of his/her specific students and the community in which she/he teaches. For example, the activities directed toward reviewing and developing decision-making skills found on page 109 may be implemented earlier if the teacher believes his/her students do not understand how to use this process. The learning activities are stated in terms of what the teacher will do, they suggest both content and teaching technique.

If the resources recommended are not available, others covering similar content may be substituted. Planning ahead will facilitate obtaining materials for the time they are needed. A complete listing of all references, including print and nonprint resources, is contained in the bibliography section. Complete addresses are provided for a number of firms and agencies whose materials are recommended in the text of the module.

MAJOR COMPETENCY A

The student can appraise the variety of responsibilities involved in being a parent.

Subcompetencies: **Page**

The student can---

MAJOR COMPETENCY: The student can appraise the variety of responsibilities involved in being a parent.

Subcompetencies	Possible Generalizations
The student can---	
---explain a parent's responsibility to provide for the physical, emotional, social, and intellectual needs of a child.	1. An understanding of the pattern of growth (physical, social, intellectual, and emotional) aids parents in providing an environment for optimum development of each child.
	2. If food, shelter, clothing, medical care, and physical safety are provided, a child's basic physical needs are met.

Learning Activities	Resources
1.0 - 6.0 ■ ○ Establish four reading centers in classroom (or library and/or instructional media center) each devoted to one area of growth, i.e., physical, intellectual, social, emotional. Give each student an assignment sheet "Patterns of Growth" (Appendix A-1) divide class into four groups, rotate groups from one center to another. Discuss, in large group, patterns of growth in children and children's needs. Place assignment sheets in student notebooks or teachers' folders for future reference.	Draper,M.,& Draper,H. <u>Caring for Children.</u> 1975. Gordon,S.,& Wollin,N. <u>Parenting: A Guide for Young People.</u> 1975. Hurlock,E. <u>Child Growth and Development.</u> 1978.
1.0 - 6.0 Read and discuss in class Maslow's hierarchy of needs. Place on bulletin board or poster a replica of Maslow's pyramid. Ask students to find pictures illustrating human needs and place on pyramid at proper level.	Ryder,V. <u>Contemporary Living.</u> 1979. Westlake,H. <u>Relationships.</u> 1972.
2.1 ○ Divide class into four groups and assign each group a specific age: 1 year old, 10 years old, 15 years old, and 20 years old. Direct each group to list the physical needs for an individual of the age assigned and who provides for these needs. Use previous assignment sheets and other references. Share reports in class, comparing how these needs and the providers change from one age to another.	Paolucci,B., Faiola,T., & Thompson,P. <u>Personal Perspectives.</u> 1978.
1.0 - 2.2 ○ After discussing basic needs in 1.0-2.1, ask students to evaluate their own needs at various stages in their lives.	

MAJOR COMPETENCY: The student can appraise the variety of responsibilities involved in being a parent.

Subcompetencies	Possible Generalizations
The student can---	
---explain a parent's responsibility to provide for the physical, emotional, social, and intellectual needs of a child.	3. If a parent helps fulfill a child's basic need for love, recognition, belonging, and achievement, the child is more likely to be emotionally secure.

Learning Activities	Resources
3.1 Show film <u>Rock-a-Bye Baby</u>. (or) Assign readings from selected resources. Discuss components of emotional security: love, recognition, belonging, and achievement, and how a parent helps provide these for children.	Film: <u>Rock-a-Bye Baby.</u> Psychology Today.
3.2 Divide class into groups and give each a role play situation. Present each role play twice: once with positive parent response, once with negative parent response. Write on the blackboard the following: a. What need does the child have in the role play? b. What are the possible results of a positive parent response? c. What are the possible results of a negative parent response? After each role play discuss the questions listed above. Suggested role plays: (1) "Hey Mom. Will you be a Den Mom? Here's a note, call Mrs. Jones. I'm gonna be a Cub Scout!" (belonging) (2) "Hey Dad, look! I got a B+ on my English paper." (achievement) (3) "Look, Mom. See the picture I painted in nursery school!" (recognition) (4) "Daddy, will you read me a story when you put me to bed?" (love) (5) "Hey, Dad. I made the junior varsity football team!" (belonging--achievement)	<u>Praise Your Children</u> and <u>Pay Attention to Your Children</u>. Southwest Educational Development Laboratory. 1976. Baker, K.R., & Fane, X.F. <u>Understanding and Guiding Young Children.</u> 1976.

MAJOR COMPETENCY: The student can appraise the variety of responsibilities involved in being a parent.

Subcompetencies	Possible Generalizations
The student can--- ---explain a parent's responsibility to provide for the physical, emotional, social, and intellectual needs of a child.	4. A child learns social expectations by experimenting with and imitating behaviors of those around him/her. 5. A child's social needs are fulfilled by the continuous interaction of the child with his/her near environment.

Learning Activities	Resources
4.1 Ask each student to bring to class a cartoon or picture showing a child imitating behavior of others or illustrating social development (or teacher may collect). Post around room. Have students discuss: ---What and how the children are learning ---Other aspects of growth and development depicted in each picture. ---Memories of their own imitating behavior.	Recommended cartoons: Dennis the Menace Family Circus Peanuts
4.2 List on blackboard games children play--for example, Simon Says. Discuss in class which and how many of these use imitation in the activity.	
4.3 Arrange for students to observe in kindergarten. Make a list of all imitating behaviors observed. Discuss in class.	
5.1 Assign students to read and define "socialization," "social environment," and "goals of socialization." Compare definitions in class and discuss similarities and differences. In groups play charades to act out terms. (or) Teacher defines terms on blackboard. Discuss in class with students providing examples to illustrate each term.	Ryder,V. <u>Contemporary Living.</u> 1979. Draper,M.,& Draper,H. <u>Caring for Children.</u> 1975. "Beyond the Front Door" and "Looking at Development," <u>Exploring Childhood.</u> 1977.

MAJOR COMPETENCY: The student can appraise the variety of responsibilities involved in being a parent.

Subcompetencies	Possible Generalizations
The student can---	
---explain a parent's responsibility to provide for the physical, emotional, social, and intellectual needs of a child.	5. A child's social needs are fulfilled by the continuous interaction of the child with his/her near environment ...continued.
	6. Development of a child's intellectual potential is influenced by his/her environment and the response of those around him/her.

Learning Activities	Resources
5.2 Around the room hang sheets of newsprint labeled baby young child, elementary-school child, adolescent, young adult, and mature adult. Give class members a set amount of time to write on each sheet all of the social environments (home, nursery school, Sunday school, friends' homes, etc.) they can list for each age group. Assign one group of students to each category. Brainstorm to list the specific goals of socialization occurring at each level. Report to class, comparing similarities and differences.	
5.3 Ask students to write a short paper describing the social growth that occurs as a child progresses through the three stages of play (or use as a discussion topic).	
6.1 Collect references on intellectual development of children. Ask students to choose a topic and write a short research paper to share with class. Possible topics: cognitive development sensory development spatial relationships Piaget's four levels of representation Bruner's goal-centered theory of learning	See preceding page.
6.2 Ask students to collect samples of children's books from home or library. In groups prepare lists of what to look for in selecting a book for a specific age level. Share in class. Discuss why it is important to read to a child or to provide books for reading.	Read to Your Child. Southwest Educational Development Laboratory. 1976.

MAJOR COMPETENCY: The student can appraise the variety of responsibilities involved in being a parent.

Subcompetencies	Possible Generalizations
The student can---	
---explain a parent's responsibility to provide for the physical, emotional, social, and intellectual needs of a child.	6. Development of a child's intellectual potential is influenced by his/her environment and the response of those around him/her...continued.

Learning Activities	Resources
6.3 Write on the blackboard: ■ Read to me Talk to me ○ Listen to me Play with me Take me to the game Hold a class debate: "Should a parenting individual say yes or no?" "Why?"	
6.4 Have students accept parenting role for a child of a specific age. Using <u>TV Guide</u> as resource, decide what programs their child could watch and state reasons for this decision. After selecting a program, have students watch it, evaluate it, and report if the decision was appropriate considering the age of the child assigned to them. (or) In small groups evaluate TV programs available for children from 6:30 p.m. to 8:00 p.m. Develop an observation worksheet for evaluating programs. Present findings to rest of school in exhibit case or bulletin board.	<u>TV Guide</u>. Radnor, Pa.: Triangle Publications, Inc.
6.5 Assign students to watch Sesame Street or Electric Company or obtain a segment to show class. Write a report on the methods used to stimulate intellectual growth of viewers. For what age child are programs designed? Divide class into small groups to review current articles in magazines and newspapers on the effect of TV on the intellectual and/or the creative growth of children.	PBS daily program produced from Children's Workshop Network.

MAJOR COMPETENCY: The student can appraise the variety of responsibilities involved in being a parent.

Subcompetencies	Possible Generalizations
The student can---	
---explain a parent's responsibility to provide for the physical, emotional, social, and intellectual needs of a child.	6. Development of a child's intellectual potential is influenced by his/her environment and the response of those around him/her...continued.
	7. The family provides the major setting for growth and development of infants and young children; in later years the setting is enlarged to include the community, the nation, and the world.

Learning Activities	Resources
1.0 - 6.0 ■ A. Copy children's needs (as compiled by student -assignment sheet A-1) each on a separate piece of paper and place in a bag or box. Direct students in turn to select a paper from box, read it aloud, and describe what a <u>parent</u> could do to provide for the need. Other students may add suggestions after first student has completed his/her statement.	
B. Have students write a short paper, "If a parent does not provide for these needs, who is responsible?"	BULLETIN BOARD:
7.1 ☐ Prepare bulletin board as suggested or in a similar way before discussion. Divide class into three groups: one to represent the community, one to represent the state/nation, and one to represent the world. Assign the groups to find information on the contribution made by each to the growth and development of children. After listing these contributions, have groups brainstorm what they would <u>like</u> each to contribute. Prepare reports or panel discussions to share with class.	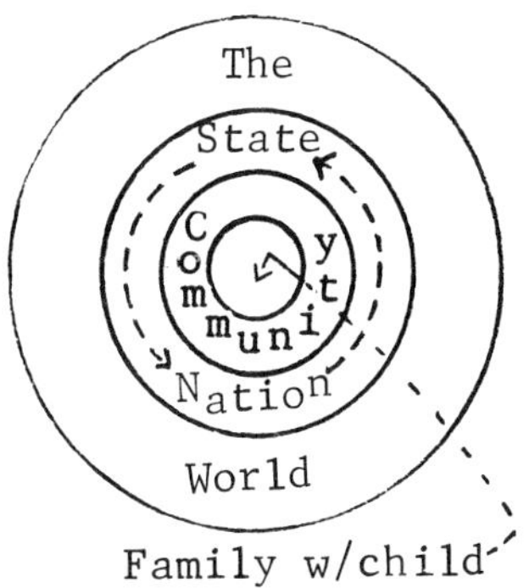 Working Together Helping Children Grow
7.2 Help students develop a family/school relationship questionnaire based on "A Community Assessment." Conduct the survey. Invite representatives from parents' groups and school administration to discuss how your community schools shape families.	"Impact on Families: A Community Assessment." <u>Forum</u>. J.C. Penney Co., Spring 1979, pp. 6-7. For 7.1: ..State and/or national legislative representative ..State council for children ..City council member or mayor or school board member ..United nations children's organization
1.0 - 7.0 Summarize with students by completing these open-ended statements: A parent fulfills a child's physical needs by.... A parent fulfills a child's emotional needs by....	

MAJOR COMPETENCY: The student can appraise the variety of responsibilities involved in being a parent.

Subcompetencies	Possible Generalizations
The student can---	
---explain a parent's responsibility to provide for the physical, emotional, social, and intellectual needs of a child.	7. The family provides the major setting for growth and development of infants and young children; in later years the setting is enlarged to include the community, the nation, and the world...continued.

Learning Activities	Resources
A parent fulfills a child's social needs by.... A parent fulfills a child's intellectual needs by.... Summarizing orally will permit correcting misconceptions and omissions. 1.0 - 7.0 ☐ Have students prepare as a project a booklet listing all agencies available in the community and the services offered for the physical, social, emotional, and intellectual needs of children. Define "community" before beginning, as you may wish to extend beyond immediate area to provide a challenging project.	

MAJOR COMPETENCY: The student can appraise the variety of responsibilities involved in being a parent.

Subcompetencies	Possible Generalizations
The student can---	
---describe what children learn from the role models provided by parenting individuals.	1. A child observes and imitates the behavior of parenting individuals.
	2. A child will learn expanded or stereotyped sex roles from parenting individuals as a result of modeling.

Learning Activities	Resources
1.1 Ask students to respond to worksheet titled "Fathers, Mothers, and Others" (Appendix A-2). Complete and hold in a file or notebook. Show filmstrip Fathers, Mothers, and Others. Discuss variety of parenting individuals depicted in strip. From responses of students on worksheet (A-3), list on blackboard all parenting individuals students mentioned, i.e., sister, brother, neighbor, etc. In the adjoining column ask students to list all individuals they have parented. Have each student write a short essay,"Who is a parent?" or prepare a collage with poetry, pictures, words, etc., with the same title.	Kit: Parenting: Fathers, Mothers, and Others. J.C. Penney Co. 1975.
1.2 Have students complete worksheet "Parts People Play" (Appendix A-3). Write a definition of parenting.	
2.1 Show film Sex Role Development.* Discuss: How do children learn from role models? How are roles changing in today's society?	Film: Sex Role Development. CRM Productions. *Alternate filmstrips: Mothers and Fathers. Set #3--"Mother/Father Roles." Parents' Magazine Films, Inc. (or) Reexamining Sex Roles: Evolution or Revolution? Sunburst Communications.
2.2 Divide class by sex. In buzz sessions, boys list for girls, girls for boys, examples of expanded sex roles and stereotyped sex roles. (Teacher may need to define each of these terms. Expanded Sex Role - both males and females are free to embrace roles that have traditionally been prescribed to one sex. Stereotyped Sex	

MAJOR COMPETENCY: The student can appraise the variety of responsibilities involved in being a parent.

Subcompetencies	Possible Generalizations
The student can---	
---describe what children learn from the role models provided by parenting individuals.	2. A child will learn expanded or stereotyped sex roles from parenting individuals as a result of modeling ...continued.
	3. A child absorbs the attitudes, aspirations, joys, anxieties, and tensions felt in the home, and will tend to give back what is received.
	4. As a result of modeling, a child can imitate negative behavior such as child abuse as well as positive behavior such as the expression of love.

Learning Activities	Resources
Roles - all males or females, because they share a common gender, also share common abilities, interests, values, and roles.) Report to class and discuss.	
2.3 Assign students to read a portion of a book or short story. Example: --Life With Father --Life With Mother --Mama's Bank Account --Cheaper By the Dozen --Others Orally contrast roles depicted with today's roles or write a short paper.	
2.4 ■ ○ Request that students find and bring to class a picture of a parenting individual in a stereotyped or expanded sex role. Write a paper, "What a Child Could Learn from This Role Model." Pictures and paragraphs could be mounted on bulletin board.	
3.1 Make transparency from "Children Learn What They Live" (Appendix A-4). Discuss implications of each item for parenting individuals. Ask students to select one item and illustrate it by describing an incident personally experienced.	Poem: "Children Learn What They Live." Appendix A-4.
4.1 Show filmstrip "The Alternatives." Discuss: ---Various ways parents express love. ---Various ways parents divide responsibilities.	Filmstrip #2: Preparation for Parenthood. Sunburst Communications.

MAJOR COMPETENCY: The student can appraise the variety of responsibilities involved in being a parent.

Subcompetencies	Possible Generalizations
The student can---	
---describe what children learn from the role models provided by parenting individuals.	4. As a result of modeling, a child can imitate negative behavior such as child abuse as well as positive behavior such as the expression of love...continued.

Learning Activities	Resources
4.2 Use second item from transparency (Appendix A-4) to stimulate discussion of child abuse. ☐	
Invite a guest speaker to discuss child abuse in general terms with specific emphasis on the abused child becoming an abusive parent.	Representative from: Social Services Parents Anonymous Police/sheriff office County attorney's office
4.3 Collect articles from newspapers and magazines--display on bulletin board. Assign report topics to individuals or groups to be shared in class. Include causes of abuse, rights of children under the law, how to report child abuse, prevention and treatment programs, and availability of hot lines. ☐ Present reports in class and discuss.	Norton, G.R. *Parenting*. 1977. Chapter 9. *Families in Stress*. National Center on Child Abuse and Neglect. Information packet--*Child Abuse*. Iowa Council for Children.
4.4 Show filmstrip "Child Abuse and Neglect." Lead short summary discussion. (or) Show film *The War of the Eggs*. Lead a short summary discussion.	Filmstrip Set #1: *Children in Crises*. Parents' Magazine Films, Inc. Film: *The War of the Eggs*. Paulist Productions.

MAJOR COMPETENCY: The student can appraise the variety of responsibilities involved in being a parent.

Subcompetencies	Possible Generalizations
The student can---	
---explain the importance of maintaining realistic expectations for child and parent.	1. Unrealistic expectations of a person's capabilities at any stage of development can hinder child or parent growth (social, emotional, intellectual, physical).

Learning Activities	Resources
1.1 Show filmstrip "Parents Expect--Children Want." ◯	Filmstrip Set #2: Conflicts between Parents and Children. Parents' Magazine Films, Inc.
Ask students if they can recall instances when they--- ---were expected to do something beyond their ability. ---expected parents to do something beyond their ability.	
Discuss feelings and conflicts that might result.	
1.2 Assign pp. 23-26 in For Every Child.	For Every Child. The Iowa Council for Children. 1978.
List factors that affect how parents' expectations for their children are (were) developed.	
Show and discuss film Forcing Children to Fail.*	Film: Forcing Children to Fail. Piaget.
	*Alternate filmstrip: Understanding Early Childhood. Set #1--"The Child's Relationship with the Family." Parents' Magazine Films, Inc.
1.3 Brainstorm: How/where can parents and/or future parents develop realistic expectations for growth and development of children?	
If not done in a previous unit, survey community to see what types of parenthood education opportunities are available for parents.	
1.4 Invite a panel of parents to discuss "Guiding growth and development of children requires parents to grow, too."	
Include parents whose children are of different ages.	

MAJOR COMPETENCY: The student can appraise the variety of responsibilities involved in being a parent.

Subcompetencies	Possible Generalizations
The student can---	
---Explain the importance of maintaining realistic expectations for child and parent.	2. A child's interests will not necessarily reflect the interests and expectations of the parent.

Learning Activities	Resources
2.1 Show and discuss filmstrip "Family Relationships - Expectations vs. Realities."	Filmstrip Set#2: Mothers and Fathers. Parents' Magazine Films, Inc.
2.2 Mount on flannel board pictures of boy/girl in varied activities: playing instrument, participating in sports, reading a book, camping, working on car. Caption on each should reflect opposite interest, e.g., boy reading book, "Bill's parents like skiing"; girl shooting basket, "Jill's parents are musicians."	
Play "Let's Pretend" (in large or small groups or through role playing).	
a. You are Bill and your parents tell you they have arranged skiing lessons for you. b. You are Bill's parents. c. You are Jill and your parents buy you a new piano. d. You are Jill's parents.	
(others appropriate to pictures available)	
Discuss:	
--Do differing interests of family members need to cause conflicts within the family? --What techniques can be used to accommodate all interests of all family members?	
Have small groups brainstorm to help Jill and her family and/or Bill and his family (or similar case studies) accommodate differences in interests within the family.	
--What are some activities or common interests families can share?	

MAJOR COMPETENCY: The student can appraise the variety of responsibilities involved in being a parent.

Subcompetencies	Possible Generalizations
The student can---	
---explain the importance of maintaining realistic expectations for child and parent.	3. A child's behavior may be characteristic of the child's age and stage of development, yet the behavior may be unacceptable to parents.
	4. Since some conflict is normal in any close relationship, parent-child conflict is normal and is to be expected.

Learning Activities	Resources
3.1 Show film <u>He Acts His Age</u>. Discuss behavior characteristics of children at different ages. Observe behavior of children of different ages: brothers and sisters, in church nursery, in day care center, etc. Ask class to prepare a simple observation form, so all will watch for similar behavior and activities. Discuss observations in class.	Film: <u>He Acts His Age</u>. McGraw-Hill Films.
3.2 Divide class into groups giving each a ◯ brief case study. Examples: a. Judy, age 6, has been told to put her toys away when she has finished playing with them. Her skates are found on the front steps. b. Paul, age 4, spills milk on the floor as he is pouring some for himself. Assign: If this behavior is not acceptable to you as a parent, what would you do?	Pamphlets from Positive Parent Early Childhood Program, S.W. Ed. Development Lab., Austin, Tex.
4.1 Assign groups to role play conflicts between parent and child. Elementary student: bedtime, practicing musical instrument, watching TV. Secondary student: request for money, using the car, staying out late. Divide class audience into two groups: a parent group and a child group. Ask each group to analyze the role plays according to the role they are assuming.	Hughes, H.M. <u>Life in Families</u>. 1970. Chapter 14.

MAJOR COMPETENCY: The student can appraise the variety of responsibilities involved in being a parent.

Subcompetencies	Possible Generalizations
The student can---	
---explain the importance of maintaining realistic expectations for child and parent.	4. Since some conflict is normal in any close relationship, parent-child conflict is normal and is to be expected...continued.

Learning Activities	Resources
4.2 Have students read resources to determine causes of conflict between parents and children. What influence does the age of a child play? Recommended: Mama Spanks Me.	Landis, J.T. & Landis, M.G. Personal Adjustment Marriage and Family Living. 1970. p. 125, 131- 32. Mama Spanks Me. Curriculum in Child Development and Family Relations. State of Iowa. 1956.

MAJOR COMPETENCY: The student can appraise the variety of responsibilities involved in being a parent.

Subcompetencies	Possible Generalizations
The student can---	
---point out the relationship between a child's rights and parent's rights.	1. A child has the right to provision of love and understanding, adequate health and social services, protection against physical and legal abuse, and freedom to express feelings and ideas of his/her own.
	2. A parent has the right to provide guidelines for the child's behavior, to express angry feelings in a constructive manner, to expect the child to understand parental limitations, and to have some privacy and time alone.
	3. Since a child's rights and a parent's rights are both important in family living, it is necessary to maintain a balance between the two.

Learning Activities	Resources
1.1 Discuss the rights of students and rights of teachers. (See school's copy of students' rights in handbook.) What is meant by "right"?	
1.2 - 2.1 - 3.1 a. Divide class into two groups: one group brainstorm rights of children, the other the rights of parents. Write on newsprint and post side by side. Search resources to find additional rights and add.	Gordon, S., and Wollin, N. <u>Parenting: A Guide for Young People</u>. 1975. Chapter 3.
(or)	
b. Post on wall a copy of "Children's Rights" from <u>Parenting</u> by Gordon and Wollin and a copy of parent's rights as follows:	<u>Children's Rights</u>. Nat. PTA. Ames, L.B. <u>Child Care and Development</u>. 1970. p. 286.
A PARENT'S RIGHTS ---To provide guidelines for a child's behavior ---To express angry feelings in a positive manner ---To expect the child to understand parental limitations ---To have some privacy and time alone	
Discuss: ---How would you balance these rights in a family? ---What problems or conflicts might arise? ---How could these conflicts be resolved?	
Summarize by writing a bill of rights for <u>families</u>.	

MAJOR COMPETENCY: The student can appraise the variety of responsibilities involved in being a parent.

Subcompetencies	Possible Generalizations
The student can---	
---point out the relationship between a child's rights and parent's rights.	4. Within the family situation the rights of week-end parents, grandparents, step parents, and others in a parenting role need to be considered.

Learning Activities	Resources
4.1 Ask class members to interview an individual from one of the following groups: grandparents, step parents, week-end parents, others in a parenting role. Ask: "As a ________________, what are your rights?" Report to class and discuss the conflicts and/or the problems these rights might cause within a family. On the blackboard list the rights expected by each group with the conflicts and problems indicated beside each. Have groups select one category and suggest possible solutions or compromises for balancing all individual rights within a family.	
1.0 - 4.0 Assign individual research topics to class members to be written or reported orally to class. Examples: a. Laws pertaining to rights and responsibilities of parents. b. Gray Panthers stand on rights of grandparents of children in divorced families. c. Developmental responsibilities of parents contrasted with legal responsibilities of parents. d. Other.	

MAJOR COMPETENCY: The student can appraise the variety of responsibilities involved in being a parent.

Subcompetencies	Possible Generalizations
The student can---	
---analyze the importance of developing and maintaining parent-child relationships.	1. Having open lines of communication is important in developing parent-child relationships.

Learning Activities	Resources
1.1 Ask students to write letters to good friends describing their relationship with their parents, including what is good and what needs to be changed. At end of unit return letter to students to see if they would like to make changes.	Norton, G.R. Parenting. 1977. Chapter 2.
1.2 Show film(s): ---What Do You Mean--What Do I Mean? (and/or) ---Many Hear and Some Listen List five facts learned about communication. Discuss other concepts presented.	Films: What Do You Mean--What Do I Mean? and Many Hear and Some Listen. Centron Films.
1.3 Have students read resources on topic parent-child communication. Role play: ---Sending I-you messages. ---Sending affectionate vs. hostile statements.	Gordon, T. Parent Effectiveness Training. 1970. Ginott, H. Between Parent and Child. 1965. "Getting Involved Working with Children." Exploring Childhood. 1977.
1.4 Give each student paper "bugs" of different colors. Write one response on each: ---What is one thing you do to "bug" family members? ---What is one thing a family member does to "bug" you? Discuss as a class: ---How does this "bugging" affect family relationships? ---Could improving communication in the family help these situations? How? Use bugs to decorate a bulletin board.	

MAJOR COMPETENCY: The student can appraise the variety of responsibilities involved in being a parent.

Subcompetencies	Possible Generalizations
The student can---	
---analyze the importance of developing and maintaining parent-child relationships.	1. Having open lines of communication is important in **developing** parent-child relationships...continued.
	2. Parent-child relationships affect the self-concept of both the parent and the child.

Learning Activities	Resources
1.5 Summarize, using circle response technique: each student in turn stating one reason communication is important in parent-child relationships.	
2.1 Define self-concept as a class.	
View filmstrip "I See Strength."	Filmstrips Set #3: <u>What Do I See When I See Me?</u> Parents' Magazine Films, Inc.
Discuss: What is the relationship of self-concept to growth and development?	
2.2 Assign students to research available resources individually or in small groups to determine how a parent can build a positive self-image in children and in themselves and how this affects parent-child relationships. Discuss findings in class.	Dodson, F. <u>How to Father</u>. 1974. Caplan, F. <u>The Parenting Advisor</u>. 1977. Yamamata, K. <u>The Child and His Image</u>. 1972. Norton, G.R. <u>Parenting</u>. 1977.
2.3 Role play using each situation twice: (1) to illustrate building negative self-concept and (2) to illustrate building positive self-concept. Possible situations: a. Four year old - "Let me bake cookies." b. "I just hit a baseball through Mr. Jones's window." c. "Read to me." d. "Dad, may I use the car tonight?" e. "Look what I made in school today!" (or) Use topics above for small group discussion topics.	

MAJOR COMPETENCY: The student can appraise the variety of responsibilities involved in being a parent.

Subcompetencies	Possible Generalizations
The student can---	
---analyze the importance of developing and maintaining parent-child relationships.	2. Parent-child relationships affect the self-concept of both the parent and the child...continued.
	3. Since parents as well as children are going through developmental stages, constant adaptation in interpersonal relationships is necessary in parent-child interaction.

Learning Activities	Resources
2.4 Have students read from resources about building self-esteem.	Simon, S. <u>I Am Lovable and Capable</u>. 1973.
● Ask students to monitor the put-downs (lowers self-esteem) and the buildups (raises self-esteem) each encounters in one day. Discuss in class student reactions to buildups and putdowns.	Satir, V. <u>Peoplemaking</u>. 1972.
Use group buzz sessions: "What can I do to help others improve their self-concept?" Consider parents, friends, grandparents, siblings, employers....	
(or)	
Write a paper: "Yesterday I improved the self-concept (or self-image or self-esteem) of ____________."	
(or)	
☐ Hold a bumper sticker writing contest directed toward improving self-image. Example: Have You Hugged Your Kid Today? For an FHA project, enlist art department and printing class to design bumper stickers, print, and distribute.	
3.1 Assign research topic - developmental stages of growth, birth through death.	
Share reports in class emphasizing that all people are continually advancing through developmental stages.	

MAJOR COMPETENCY: The student can appraise the variety of responsibilities involved in being a parent.

Subcompetencies	Possible Generalizations
The student can---	
---analyze the importance of developing and maintaining parent-child relationships.	3. Since parents as well as children are going through developmental stages, constant adaptation in interpersonal relationships is necessary in parent-child interaction...continued.
	4. Since no two children nor parents are alike, parent-child relationships will have different dimensions with each child and parent in the family.

Learning Activities	Resources
3.2 Discuss developmental stages in class in terms of how these might affect parent-child interaction in the following families: --- Tom and Jean: 23-28 - Jim aged 5 --- Ann and David: 35-43 - Kirk 6 months Steve 17 years	Landis, J.T., & Landis, M.G. *Personal Adjustment, Marriage and Family Living*. 1972. Westlake, H. *Relationships*. 1972. "Developmental Stages for Adults." Appendix A-5.
4.1 Have students interview parents who have more than one child. (Include if possible the parents of twins.) Ask: --- In what ways are your children alike? --- In what ways are they different? --- How do these similarities and differences affect your relationship with each child? and between each child? Discuss results of survey in class and implications for parenting.	Havighurst, R. *Developmental Tasks*. 1974.
4.2 Assign students to write discussion papers answering the following questions: --- Are your parents' expectations the same for you as for your brothers and sisters? --- What are the differences and why do they exist? --- How does this affect family relationships? (This may lead to a discussion of sibling rivalry. If so, show film *Jamie: Story of a Sibling*.) Encourage several students to share and discuss their papers with the class.	Film: *Jamie: Story of a Sibling*. McGraw-Hill Films.

MAJOR COMPETENCY: The student can appraise the variety of responsibilities involved in being a parent.

Subcompetencies	Possible Generalizations
The student can---	
---analyze the importance of developing and maintaining parent-child relationships.	5. Since mutual respect and understanding are bases for maintaining positive parent-child relationships, it is necessary for both parent and child to work toward these.
	6. The quality of the parent-child relationship influences the development of children.

Learning Activities	Resources
5.1 Show filmstrip "Memories." Discuss: --- What qualities do you possess that you would like to see in your future child(ren)? --- What qualities do you possess that you would not like to see in your future child(ren)? Ask each student to list three things parents did for them that-- --- they will do for their child(ren). --- they will not do for their child(ren).	Filmstrip #3: <u>Preparation for Parenthood</u>. Sunburst Communications.
5.2 Ask students to respond to open ended questions (in writing or orally): --- I respect my parents the most when ____________. --- My parents respect me the most when ____________. --- I do not understand my parents when ____________. --- My parents do not understand me when ____________. Summarize.	
6.1 Assign students to read a book or short story or watch a TV show* that involves parent-child relationships. Look for contrast in quality of relationships--good vs. poor. Report: --- Brief synopsis of story Was the self-image of parent and/or child improved or damaged as a result of the relationship depicted	*or have AEA videotape a show and use it in class.

MAJOR COMPETENCY: The student can appraise the variety of responsibilities involved in being a parent.

Subcompetencies	Possible Generalizations
The student can---	
---analyze the importance of developing and maintaining parent-child relationships.	6. The quality of the parent-child relationship influences the development of children...continued.

Learning Activities	Resources
---How could this relationship influence the development of the child and/or the parent? Discuss reports in class.	

MAJOR COMPETENCY: The student can appraise the variety of responsibilities involved in being a parent.

Subcompetencies	Possible Generalizations
The student can---	
---assess the implications of the economic factors of raising a child.	1. Parents are legally responsible for the economic support of a child until the age of eighteen.
	2. The economic cost of raising a child to maturity is conservatively estimated to be $2\frac{1}{2}$ times the family's annual income at the time of the child's birth.

Learning Activities	Resources
1.1 Have a resource person from the Department of Social Services in your community or county discuss the legal responsibilities parents have for the economic support of their children.	
1.2 Do a class presentation on the legal responsibilities of parents to their children. (or) Prepare summaries of legislative acts. Divide class into groups. Give each group a summary of a different legislative act. Have groups prepare a class presentation on the act they were given. These presentations should emphasize the responsibilities parents have. (Provide newsprint, markers , transparencies, etc.)	
2.1 Show filmstrip "Laying the Groundwork." Discuss: ----When are people financially ready to have a child? --- What are some of the costs involved in raising a child?	Filmstrip #1: The Economics of Parenthood. Parents' Magazine Films, Inc.
2.2 Gather the following items and place them around the room: a. Recent articles and/or books on the costs of raising children such as "What It Takes to Raise a Child" or Sylvia Porter's Money Book.	"What It Takes to Raise a Child." Money. Sept. 1975. P. 25.

MAJOR COMPETENCY: The student can appraise the variety of responsibilities involved in being a parent.

Subcompetencies	Possible Generalizations
The student can---	
---assess the implications of the economic factors of raising a child.	2. The economic cost of raising a child to maturity is conservatively estimated to be $2\frac{1}{2}$ times the family's annual income at the time of the child's birth...continued.

Learning Activities	Resources
b. List of a few area doctors and their prenatal and postnatal care fees. c. List required immunizations for children and costs. d. Suggested lists of baby equipment from magazines and/or child development text. e. Catalogues from stores such as Sears, Wards, J.C. Penney. f. Current prices for baby food and formula. g. List of child care facilities and costs.	Porter, S. Sylvia Porter's Money Book. 1975. Pp. 58-68, 697-712. Clark, L.E. The Cost and Value of American Children. 1977.
Draw a lifeline for a child from birth to age 18 on the blackboard. Have students list items needed at each age. Assign each student an age and have the student investigate the cost of the items listed for that age. Have students suggest alternative ways of providing these items and the comparable costs in terms of time and money. Examples: second hand or used furniture, garage sales, hand-me-downs, Salvation Army, Goodwill, etc. (Students can use the materials around the room and should be encouraged to also use additional references and/or materials.)	
2.3 Set up four learning centers around the room. Put each of the following filmstrips and appropriate discussion questions in each learning center: "Nine Months to Get Ready" "Now There are Three" "Baby Begins to Grow" "It's Time for School" Have students rotate among the learning centers.	Filmstrips #2-5: The Economics of Parenthood. Parents' Magazine Films, Inc.

(or)

MAJOR COMPETENCY: The student can appraise the variety of responsibilities involved in being a parent.

Subcompetencies	Possible Generalizations
The student can---	
---assess the implications of the economic factors of raising a child.	2. The economic cost of raising a child to maturity is conservatively estimated to be 2½ times the family's annual income at the time of the child's birth...continued.
	3. Raising a child may cause the loss of one or both parents' income either temporarily or permanently.

Learning Activities	Resources
Have each group develop a class presentation on the economic costs of parenthood presented in the filmstrip its group viewed. Discuss the costs that remain the same and those that change as a child grows. 3.1 Have students develop a questionnaire or provide a questionnaire for students to administer to parents asking if both parents worked prior to the birth of a child, after the baby came, if they are working now, etc. Include questions on: --- Maternity leave provided by employer --- Health insurance --- What effects these decisions regarding both parents working had on the family's lifestyle (i.e., the kinds of activities engaged in, amount of money available for recreation, etc.) Have each student administer questionnaire to three parents in the community. Tabulate results and discuss implications. 3.2 ☐ Panel of Parents Activity. Invite couples where both parents are employed, couples where only one parent is employed, and a single parent to participate in a panel discussion. Have the students develop questions on why the parents on the panel made their respective decisions (economics, career goals, child care facilities available, costs of child care, etc.).	

MAJOR COMPETENCY: The student can appraise the variety of responsibilities involved in being a parent.

Subcompetencies	Possible Generalizations
The student can---	
---assess the implications of the economic factors of raising a child.	4. If both parents are wage earners, in addition to providing for food, shelter, clothing and education, they also have to provide care facilities for the child during times when they are unable to perform this task.
	5. Providing for the expenses of child-rearing may restrict or limit the amount of money available for social and educational opportunities of the parents.

Learning Activities	Resources
4.1 Divide the class into groups. Give each group a pamphlet on choosing care for children. (Each group will have a different type of care facility). Have the group summarize the major characteristics of that type of facility and the relative advantages and disadvantages. Types of care facilities available include: a. Family day care homes b. Day care-child care center c. Preschool or nursery school d. A babysitter in your home e. Play groups f. Babysitting 'ooperatives Have the groups determine whether the type of care facility they had is available in their community. If it is available, have them research the costs. Have groups share and discuss their findings.	Pinskey,D. <u>Choosing Care for Your Child</u>. 1977-78.
4.2 Use "Voice a Choice" activity from J.C. Penney Kit on Parenting. Choose a care center to best meet the needs of each of the four family situations presented.	<u>Parenting: Fathers, Mothers, and Others</u>. J.C. Penney.
5.1 Prepare budgets for three different families (2 career, 1 career, single person, etc.) using the handout "Your Budget--Can You Afford a Child?" (Appendix A-6) Divide the class into groups and give each group one of the budgets. Have groups decide if the family can afford a child. What activities will they have to limit if they decide to have a child? Share group findings. Help students draw conclusions on how the decision to have a child influences the money available for other activities. Draw comparisons between the families represented.	

MAJOR COMPETENCY B

The student can utilize the decision-making process in determining if and when to become a parent.

Subcompetencies: Page

The student can---

MAJOR COMPETENCY: The student can utilize the decision-making process in determining if and when to become a parent.

Subcompetencies	Possible Generalizations
The student can---	
---recognize that parenthood is optional.	1. The availability of information on family planning may enable one to control childbearing.
	2. In today's society the traditional form of marriage that includes parenting is only one of several choices available to individuals.

Learning Activities	Resources
1.1 Make available in the classroom leaflets and articles dealing with birth control. Have students examine materials and write down questions they may have about birth control methods.	Family Planning resources from Planned Parenthood. The Hassles of Becoming a Teenage Parent. DHEW Publication No. (HSA)78-5624.
1.2 Invite community resource person such as a gynecologist or family planning specialist (e.g., from Planned Parenthood) to present information on family planning to class. Use students' questions as a basis for content of presentation. To further clarify students' questions, have follow-up discussion in subsequent class session.	Westlake, H.G. Relationships. 1972. pp. 327-37.
2.1 Have students complete opinionnaire "What Do You Think?" (Appendix B-1). Lead class in discussion of each question, seeking to raise consciousness of students in regard to parenting.	
2.2 Divide class into groups. Have half the groups prepare posters (or collages) that represent the traditional form of marriage and parenting (nuclear family, mother as homemaker, father as financial provider). Have remainder of the groups work on posters that show varying forms of marriages (and cohabitation) and parenting. Some of these varying forms may include: --- Single parent (man or woman) ----Dual career family (with or without children) ----Single career family where wife is financial provider --- Couple who live together and have children	Westlake, H.G. Relationships. 1972. Chapters 22, 23, and 27. Craig, H.T. Thresholds to Adult Living. 1976. Pp. 261-67.

MAJOR COMPETENCY: The student can utilize the decision-making process in determining if and when to become a parent.

Subcompetencies	Possible Generalizations
The student can---	
---recognize that parenthood is optional.	2. In today's society the traditional form of marriage that includes parenting is only one of several choices available to individuals ...continued.
	3. Many couples are choosing childlessness as an alternative to parenting.

Learning Activities	Resources
--- Grandparents or other relatives rearing children --- Foster parents Have groups share posters with each other. Discuss.	
3.1 Show film <u>You Can't Mean Not Ever</u>.	Film: <u>You Can't Mean Not Ever</u>. University of Minnesota. 1977.
3.2 Have students list possible reasons why a couple may choose not to have children. Discuss.	
3.3 Have students role play the following case situation (or an adapted version that reflects your community): Karen and Tim, both in their late twenties, have recently married. They are trying to make a decision about parenthood. Karen teaches school and Tim manages a clothing store. While both like children, they are not certain if they want to be parents. Karen is particularly concerned about interrupting her teaching career. What are some of the alternatives they may discuss? Some possible alternatives: a. Remain childless, discussing the fact that children may not fit their lifestyle. b. Have children, but equally share parenting role so that both can continue careers. c. "Parent" relatives (e.g., nieces, nephews) or children of friends. Become active in "Big Brother" and "Big Sister" programs.	Craig,H.T. <u>Threshold to Adult Living</u>. 1976. Pp. 253-54.

MAJOR COMPETENCY: The student can utilize the decision-making process in determining if and when to become a parent.

Subcompetencies	Possible Generalizations
The student can---	
---recognize that parenthood is optional.	3. Many couples are choosing childlessness as an alternative to parenting ...continued.

Learning Activities	Resources
d. Become foster parents and keep children on a temporary basis. Discuss alternatives, stressing that childlessness is one possible option.	

MAJOR COMPETENCY: The student can utilize the decision-making process in determining if and when to become a parent.

Subcompetencies	Possible Generalizations
The student can---	
---recognize the need to make a decision about whether or not to become a parent.	1. As parenthood is optional, one needs to make decisions about whether or not to become a parent.
	2. Examining possible choices and the consequences of each may aid one in making a decision about becoming a parent.

Learning Activities	Resources
1.1 Have students complete "The Egg" experience. (Although the objectives are the same, plants or china dishes can be substituted for eggs.) As a follow-up activity, have students write a paper relating the experience of parenting at this time in their lives. Based on the experience, have students make the decision of whether or not they feel they are ready to become a parent.	Fisher,R.M. "Eggs Help Teach Responsibility." Illinois Teacher. 1976. P. 139. Kloosterhouse,V. "Trying on Parenthood." What's New in Home Economics. 1978. P. LP-1--LP-4.
2.1 Have students sit in a circle. Introduce the following case situation for discussion: Joe and Valerie, both 20 years old, are sophomores in college and have been married for one year. They are trying to decide whether to have a child now or wait until both have finished school. Both have scholarships to pay major school expenses but work part-time to pay nonschool costs and add to their savings. Valerie is majoring in retailing and will be able to secure a job following graduation. Joe, however, wants to go to law school upon completing his degree. Have students list the possible choices or alternatives Joe and Valerie may have. (List on chalkboard.) Some possible choices may include: a. Have child now. b. Have child when both have finished college. c. Wait until Joe has finished law school. d. Wait until both have become established in their careers.	

MAJOR COMPETENCY: The student can utilize the decision-making process in determining if and when to become a parent.

Subcompetencies	Possible Generalizations
The student can---	
---recognize the need to make a decision about whether or not to become a parent.	2. Examining possible choices and the consequences of each may aid one in making a decision about becoming a parent...continued.
	3. A couple is ready to have a child only when both really want it and have faced ramifications in the relationship that result from its coming.

Learning Activities	Resources
Taking each choice or alternative at a time, go around circle and have students give a consequence for that choice. Students who cannot think of a consequence may "pass." Once all choices have been examined, lead discussion concerning importance of "choices and consequences" in making a decision regarding parenthood. This activity can be repeated, using different case situations. 3.1 Have students role play the following case situation: Julie and Fred have been married for three years. While Julie always thought she wanted children, she is now having second thoughts since her career as an interior designer is quite demanding. Fred, an insurance agent, has always felt that a family is not complete without children. What are some issues this couple will have to resolve in making the decision about parenthood? How might their relationship be affected by the decision? Some possible issues: a. Interruption of Julie's career. b. Clarification of Julie and Fred's feelings about children in relation to family life; clarification of role expectations. c. Role reversal (Fred as major care giver). d. Dual role (equally sharing parenting role).	

MAJOR COMPETENCY: The student can utilize the decision-making process in determining if and when to become a parent.

Subcompetencies	Possible Generalizations
The student can---	
---recognize the need to make a decision about whether or not to become a parent.	3. A couple is ready to have a child only when both really want it and have faced ramifications in the relationship that result from its coming...continued.
	4. Making a conscious decision to become a parent helps to eliminate the stress associated with an unplanned pregnancy.

Learning Activities	Resources
Effects on relationship: a. Fred may be resentful if they do not have children. b. Julie may be bitter if her career is interrupted to have children. c. In having children Julie may perceive unforeseen advantages, and Fred may see disadvantages of parenthood. d. Fred and Julie may have ambivalent or conflicting feelings toward children that may affect their relationship.	
4.1 Have students read "Lynn's Story" from <u>Inside Your Body, Inside Your Head</u> (Appendix B-2). Discuss how her unplanned pregnancy caused stress on herself and others. Have students rewrite story, with Lynn making a conscious decision regarding parenthood. Discuss with students: What changes did you make in Lynn's life before she was ready to make a conscious decision about parenthood?	<u>Inside Your Body, Inside Your Head</u>. National Foundation--March of Dimes. 1978. P. 7.

MAJOR COMPETENCY: The student can utilize the decision-making process in determining if and when to become a parent.

Subcompetencies	Possible Generalizations
The student can---	
---explain factors that influence one's decision to become a parent.	1. People may have children for a variety of reasons--emotional, spiritual, social, physical, mental and economic.
	2. Conditions in society (i.e., overpopulation, world food crisis, economic crisis, high divorce rates, increase in crime, child abuse) may influence one's decision to parent.

Learning Activities	Resources
1.1 Lead discussion on "What is a value?" Involve students in a preliminary value clarification technique. Then, as a group, have students identify values that are important in making a decision to become a parent. After list of values has been made, have students write down the following categories: emotional, spiritual, social, physical, mental and economic. Have students categorize values. Discuss: --- The variety of values that might influence the decision to parent. --- How values are important in decision making.	Simon, S., Howe, L., Kirschenbaum, H. Values Clarification. 1972.
1.2 Have each student administer "Parenting Questionnaire" (Appendix B-3) to at least five adults. Adults chosen for the survey should be of different ages (including some older adults) with children of different ages, different number of children, and with different lifestyles. Have students analyze questionnaires for "reasons for having children."	
2.1 Show filmstrip "The Decision." Following the filmstrip, have students divide into buzz groups and compile a list of societal factors that a person may consider when making a decision about parenthood. Have students report back to class, compiling a list of factors to be considered.	Filmstrip #1: Preparation for Parenthood. Sunburst Communications.

MAJOR COMPETENCY: The student can utilize the decision-making process in determining if and when to become a parent.

Subcompetencies	Possible Generalizations
The student can---	
---explain factors that influence one's decision to become a parent.	2. Conditions in society (i.e., overpopulation, world food crisis, economic crisis, high divorce rates, increase in crime, child abuse) may influence one's decision to parent...continued.
	3. The sacrifices involved in raising a child along with the satisfactions one anticipates from parenthood may influence one's decision to become a parent.

Learning Activities	Resources
2.2 Lead students in making a list of societal conditions that might affect the decision to parent. Write them on blackboard. Some possible societal conditions might include: ----Overpopulation --- World food crisis --- Economic crisis (e.g., inflation) --- High divorce rates --- Increase in crime --- Child abuse On an individual basis, have students analyze each societal condition to determine whether or not it would have an influence on their decision to parent. Have students give reasons for their answers. Discuss.	
3.1 Have students do group reports on the sacrifices one makes when raising a child. Assign each group to different areas such as time, energy, money, freedom, and aspirations. Students may use current articles, short stories, textbooks, or interviews with parents to compile reports.	Landis, J.T., & Landis, M.G. <u>Personal Adjustment, Marriage and Family Living</u>. 1970. Pp. 341-43.
3.2 Divide class into buzz groups. Have groups discuss satisfactions they would have as a result of parenthood. Have groups report back to class. Compile a class list of anticipated satisfactions.	Landis, J.T., & Landis, M.G. <u>Personal Adjustment Marriage and Family Living</u>. 1970. P. 341.
3.3 As a summary activity, lead students in compiling a list of satisfactions and sacrifices one may experience as a result of parenthood. Write list on blackboard in columns titled <u>satisfactions</u> and <u>sacrifices</u>. Discuss.	

MAJOR COMPETENCY: The student can utilize the decision-making process in determining if and when to become a parent.

Subcompetencies	Possible Generalizations
The student can---	
---explain factors that influence one's decision to become a parent.	3. The sacrifices involved in raising a child,along with the satisfactions one anticipates from parenthood,may influence one's decision to become a parent...continued.
	4. A consideration of inheritable diseases and personal health may influence one when deciding whether or not to parent.
	5. Education for parenthood may influence one's decision about whether or not to become a parent.

Learning Activities	Resources
3.4 Have students read and react to "Baby Bill of Rights." Discuss: ---What satisfactions of parenthood are reflected in the Bill of Rights? ---What realistic (and somewhat unrewarding) aspects of parenthood are reflected in the Bill of Rights?	Inside Your Body, Inside Your Head. National Foundation--March of Dimes. 1978. P. 28.
3.5 Have students analyze "Parenting Questionnaire" (Appendix B-3) for satisfactions regarding parenthood. Discuss: ---How do respondents' satisfactions compare with students list of anticipated satisfactions?	
4.1 Show filmstrip "Tomorrow Happens Today."	"Tomorrow Happens Today." March of Dimes Films.
4.2 Have students role play the following case situation: Martha and Warren have been dating for 8 months and are considering marriage. Due to the seriousness of their relationship, Warren has decided to tell Martha that an undesirable inheritable condition runs in his family. How might Martha react to this news?	Craig, H.T. Thresholds to Adult Living. 1976. Pp. 254-56.
5.1 Share the following case situations with students: a. Beverly and Paul are high school seniors who are considering marriage and children. Both are the youngest in their families. While Beverly has had some babysitting experience, Paul has had limited contact with small children.	Landis, J.T., & Landis, M.G. Personal Adjustment, Marriage and Family Living. 1970. Pp. 343-47.

MAJOR COMPETENCY: The student can utilize the decision-making process in determining if and when to become a parent.

Subcompetencies	Possible Generalizations
The student can--- ---explain factors that influence one's decision to become a parent.	5. Education for parenthood may influence one's decision about whether or not to become a parent...continued. 6. The parenting role models a person has observed and believes s/he can provide may affect the decision to parent.

Learning Activities	Resources
b. Linda and Eugene are college seniors who are considering marriage and children. Linda is the oldest in her family. Eugene is an only child but has worked part-time as a teacher's assistant in a local child care center. Both Linda and Eugene had a child development course in high school. Divide students into buzz groups and have them compare the couple's readiness for parenthood in terms of their prior educational experiences.	
6.1 Show filmstrip "Memories."	Filmstrip #3: Preparation for Parenthood. Sunburst Communications.
6.2 Lead discussion concerning parenting role models students have observed. Will students want to imitate or avoid these role models if they decide to parent a child?	

MAJOR COMPETENCY: The student can utilize the decision-making process in determining if and when to become a parent.

Subcompetencies	Possible Generalizations
The student can---	
---analyze factors that teenagers need to consider before making a decision about whether or not to become a parent.	1. A decision to become an adolescent parent affects not only the individuals directly involved but also relatives, the community, and society.
	2. In comparing pregnancy in adolescence and adulthood, adolescent pregnancy is more likely to result in low birth weight babies, birth injury, retardation and illness and/or death of the child in its first year(s).
	3. Complications in pregnancy and delivery are a greater threat to teenagers, who are twice as likely to die after a miscarriage or hemorrhage as women aged 20 to 34.
	4. Since adolescence is a time of social development, it is important to realize the effects of parenthood on the ability to be involved in social and recreational activities.

Learning Activities	Resources
1.1 - 7.1 Show films Woman-Child and Teenage Father.	Films: Woman-Child and Teenage Father. March of Dimes Films. Also available from Children's Home Society of California, 5449 McConnell Ave., Los Angeles, CA. 90066.
1.1 - 4.1 Have students complete "Strategy 4--Learning Centers" (Appendix B-5). Discuss: ---What are the effects of adolescent pregnancy on the individuals? On others?	Nye,F.I. School-Age Parenthood. 1978.
1.2 - 4.2 Have students role play the following case situation: Sharon and Tom are high school juniors who have been going steady for two years. Six months ago, they became sexually active, but have not taken precautions to prevent pregnancy. What are some of the consequences a pregnancy now would have on Sharon? On Tom? For the role playing, have students sit in a circle. Place two chairs in the middle of the circle, one labeled "Sharon" and the other "Tom." Have students take turns playing the roles of Sharon and Tom, "thinking out loud" the consequences of pregnancy.	
4.3 Have students read and discuss "Teen Marriage." How do these two cases illustrate possible outcomes for Sharon and Tom (in learning activity 1.2-4.2)?	Fooner,A. "Teen Marriage." Co-ed, Sept. 1977, pp. 77, 106.

MAJOR COMPETENCY: The student can utilize the decision-making process in determining if and when to become a parent.

Subcompetencies	Possible Generalizations
The student can---	
---analyze factors that teenagers need to consider before making a decision about whether or not to become a parent.	4. Since adolescence is a time of social development, it is important to realize the effects of parenthood on the ability to be involved in social and recreational activities...continued.
	5. Adolescent pregnancy may interrupt or prevent educational and career plans.
	6. Adolescent couples who become parents face a number of stresses and, if they marry, are more likely to have marital problems.
	7. Adolescents who become parents often find themselves unable to fit into either the adult or teenage world.

Learning Activities	Resources
4.4 ○ Have students develop an opinionnaire from Am I Parent Material pamphlet or use questions from article, "Don't Kid Yourself--Are You Ready for Parenthood?" Have students respond to opinionnaire. Discuss each question with class, noting varying opinions of class members.	Am I Parent Material? National Alliance for Optional Parenthood. Appendix B-7. Marks, J. "Don't Kid Yourself--Are You Ready for Parenthood?" Teen Magazine. May 1979, p. 124.
5.1 ● Invite to class two or three couples who are (or were) teenage parents. Have them share some advantages and disadvantages associated with teenage pregnancy. (As a substitute for this activity, students could be divided into groups and each group could interview a teenage couple who are parents.)	
5.1 - 7.1 Have students read and discuss reactions to "Teenage Parenthood: A Web of Heartaches" (Appendix B-6).	Craig, F. "Teenage Parenthood: A Web of Heartaches." Des Moines Sunday Register, November 12, 1978.
1.1 - 7.1 □ F H A encounter or class projects: a. Sponsor a "Parenting Forum," involving resource speakers, young men and women, and parents. b. Coordinate a resource center or parenting in the library or home economics department. c. Prepare puppet shows on teenage pregnancy. d. Start a parenting hotline for school and/or community.	Healthy Babies: Chance or Choice. Maryland Association, Future Homemakers of America. Maryland PP & AD Center, 1815 Woodside Avenue, Baltimore, Md. 21227.

MAJOR COMPETENCY: The student can utilize the decision-making process in determining if and when to become a parent.

Subcompetencies	Possible Generalizations
The student can---	
---determine the outcomes of the decision to become a parent at different stages of an individual's life.	1. The arrival of a child results in an irrevocable change in the life of an individual.
	2. Disruption of established lifestyles may be a cost of becoming a parent.

Learning Activities	Resources
1.1 Tape record a young child crying, constantly asking questions, making happy sounds, or an older child's temper tantrum for at least five minutes. Play the tape for the students and ask them the following questions: How would you react if you were babysitting? If you were the parent? How are the feelings similar and/or different?	
2.1 Show filmstrip "The Growing Parent". Have students discuss variety in lifestyles and the possible implications of parenthood.	Filmstrip Set #2: Understanding Parenthood. Parents' Magazine Films, Inc.
2.2 Have each student design a collage to represent the type of life style he/she would like to have. After the students present and discuss their collages, have pictures of babies cut out to paste in the middle of each. Ask each student to write a short paper describing how the new baby would disrupt his/her life style. Use the collages for display with papers attached.	Am I Parent Material? National Alliance for Optional Parenthood. Appendix B-7. Other available texts that address lifestyles.
2.3 Ask students to describe the ways in which the life style of the couple in the following case study might be disrupted. Bill and Mary had wanted a child, but after a number of years had decided that they could not have children. Both became involved in careers, an active social life, and extended vacations in other countries. Yesterday Mary went to the doctor for an annual checkup and discovered she was pregnant.	

MAJOR COMPETENCY: The student can utilize the decision-making process in determining if and when to become a parent.

Subcompetencies	Possible Generalizations
The student can---	
---determine the outcomes of the decision to become a parent at different stages of an individual's life.	3. The age of an individual and stage in life affect the decision made on whether or not to parent.
	4. Delaying parenthood can result in attainment of educational and/or career goals.

Learning Activities	Resources
3.1 Have students read selected references on developmental tasks, or review material if discussed earlier.	Havighurst, R. <u>Developmental Tasks</u>. 1974. "Developmental Stages for Adults." Appendix A-6.
3.2 Divide the class into small groups and discuss the following questions: How would life be different for you if you had a baby now? Early in marriage? Later in marriage? How do you think it would affect your life economically, mentally, emotionally, physically, and socially?	
3.3 Divide the class into four groups and assign the following group project. Each group will take one age group and collect data on the effects of becoming a parent at different ages (teens, 20's, 30's, 40's). Have each group discuss how the age affects income, social life, education, careers, health, and life styles. Reports are to be done in chart form (Appendix B-8) and summarized for the class. Encourage the students to point out similarities, differences, advantages, and disadvantages of parenting for each age group.	Textbooks, pamphlets, and articles on parenting. Interviews with parents who are in the various age groups.
4.1 Refer to activities in 3.3 above.	
4.2 ☐ Have groups of students interview teachers at the school, doctors, lawyers, or other professionals in the community to determine if they did or did not delay parenthood until they had completed preparations for their present career. Ask for their reasons for doing so, and the advantages and disadvantages of their decisions for themselves and their children. Present findings to the entire class.	

MAJOR COMPETENCY: The student can utilize the decision-making process in determining if and when to become a parent.

Subcompetencies	Possible Generalizations
The student can---	
---determine the outcomes of the decision to become a parent at different stages of an individual's life.	4. Delaying parenthood can result in attainment of educational and/or career goals...continued.
	5. Women who become pregnant after age 35 experience more health problems (maternal mortality, fetal deaths, infant mortality).

Learning Activities	Resources
4.3 List on the blackboard the reasons people do and do not delay parenthood, and give some of the advantages and disadvantages of each decision. Encourage students to discuss personal feelings concerning this topic.	
5.1 Have students collect and review articles, pamphlets, and books on the health problems associated with pregnancy at different ages (teens, 20's, 30's, and 40's).	Pamphlets, journals, health books, and family life texts.
5.2 Invite a doctor or nurse to come to class and discuss the effects of pregnancy on men and women at different ages. Encourage students to develop questions to ask the resource person.	
5.3 As a summary, have students use their notes from the readings and the information gained from the resource person to determine the age group that has the least health problems associated with it during pregnancy. For example: Ask students to rate the following age groups to indicate the best time to become pregnant as it relates to health problems: Age Groups 40's 20's teens 30's Ask students to write a short statement to justify their priority arrangement.	

MAJOR COMPETENCY: The student can utilize the decision-making process in determining if and when to become a parent.

Subcompetencies	Possible Generalizations
The student can---	
---relate the factors involved in planning short- and long-term goals regarding parenthood.	1. Progress in family planning has made it possible for a couple to set long- and short-term goals regarding parenthood.
	2. Parenting goals are affected by goals in other areas, e.g., work or career, family, friends, community, and religion.
	3. Information on (a) stages of child development, (b) behaviors expected at different stages and (c) how reacting and interacting with children influences an individual's parenting goals.

Learning Activities	Resources
1.1 Direct students to list their short term personal goals and their long term personal goals. Ask one or two class members to share personal goals with the class. As a group, analyze how becoming a parent now would affect the attainment of these goals. Discuss.	Westlake, H. Relationships. 1969. Pp. 329-36.
1.2 Assign groups in the class to research a variety of topics related to family planning. Example: Planned Parenthood Agency--how can this agency help individuals in setting and achieving long-and short-term parenting goals?	
2.1 Request students to interview parents to determine if their goals in parenting are (were) influenced by friends, career aspirations, family, religion, or community responsibilities. Try to include parents in their 20's, 30's, 40's, and older. Share results of the interviews in class and discuss. Did the age of the parenting individuals seem to affect their responses?	
3.1 Have students read and discuss selected references on the developmental stages of children. (or) Review this material if studied previously.	Dolloff, R., & Resnik, M. Patterns of Life: Human Growth and Development. 1972.

MAJOR COMPETENCY: The student can utilize the decision-making process in determining if and when to become a parent.

Subcompetencies	Possible Generalizations
The student can---	
---relate the factors involved in planning short- and long-term goals regarding parenthood.	3. Information on (a) stages of child development, (b) behaviors expected at different stages and (c) how to reacting and interacting with children influences an individual's parenting goals...continued.
	4. Changing sex roles and responsibilities makes it increasingly more important for both men and women to consider how children fit in with their other goals.
	5. Planning one's short- and long-term goals for parenting involves the timing of the first child, the total number of children in the family, and the spacing of children.

Learning Activities	Resources
3.2 Assign a specific age or ages to different groups and have them research the developmental tasks and characteristics for that age. Discuss findings.	Hurlock, E. <u>Child Growth and Development</u>. 1978.
3.3 Have students list their anticipated plans for parenting and give a reason for these plans. Discuss: ---Are the differences in plans related to amount of knowledge and/or experiences individuals have had with children? ---Why might knowledge of and experience with children be a factor in planning goals regarding parenthood?	Havighurst, R. <u>Developmental Tasks</u>. 1974.
4.1 Show filmstrip "The Growing Parent. Discuss implications of changing roles of men and women in society. (or)	Filmstrip Set #2: <u>Understanding Parenthood</u>. Parents' Magazine Films, Inc.
Ask students to read current articles on changing roles of men and women. Discuss implications these changes may have for parenting.	Cross, A. <u>Enjoying Family Living</u>. 1967. Chapter 2. Dodson, F. <u>How to Father</u>. 1974.
4.2 Have students role play a young married couple with a new baby. Illustrate current changes in male and female roles as they relate to child rearing, careers, and homemaking responsibilities.	
5.1 Refer to learning experiences 1.3 and 2.3. Have students discuss with their parents, relatives, or other parents how spacing the births of children helped them (if at all) reach short- and long-term goals.	

MAJOR COMPETENCY: The student can utilize the decision-making process in determining if and when to become a parent.

Subcompetencies	Possible Generalizations
The student can---	
---select procedures for implementing short- and long-term plans to reach parenting goals.	1. Setting priorities allows one to identify short-term and long-term plans.
	2. The use of available resources, personal and community, enables one to achieve plans.

Learning Activities	Resources
1.1 Have each student write five things they want to do in the next five years. Ask students to arrange the items in the order they hope to accomplish the plans. Help students identify the plans to be accomplished first as short-term and the ones to be accomplished later as long-term plans.	
1.2 List on the blackboard several examples of parenting plans. Encourage students to add others. Assist students in classifying the plans as long-term or short-term. Examples: --- Save for a child's college education. --- Give a birthday party for a child next month. --- Take a child to a dental appointment. --- Enroll a child in a summer camp. --- Start a family (have a baby) in two years. Point out how determining short- and long-term plans results from setting priorities.	
2.1 Divide the class into groups and have each group survey the community for people, agencies, or organizations that one could use in achieving the long- and short-term plans discussed in 1.2. Have each group report findings to the class and as a class compile a directory of community resources that could aid one to achieve parenting plans. Examples: free clinics, hotlines, services for the handicapped, genetic counseling facilities, planned parenthood centers, March of Dimes chapters, prenatal services.	

MAJOR COMPETENCY: The student can utilize the decision-making process in determining if and when to become a parent.

Subcompetencies	Possible Generalizations
The student can---	
---select procedures for implementing short- and long-term plans to reach parenting goals.	3. As unexpected events or opportunities may cause one to alter plans for achievement of goals, plans need to be flexible.

Learning Activities	Resources
3.1 Have students react to situations similar to the following by discussing ways they would try to solve the problem in each situation. Ask student to point out the possible alternatives and consequences they would consider for each situation. Also use these situations to illustrate the importance of having flexible plans.	

Situation 1

● You and your boyfriend are both juniors in college and plan to marry a year after you graduate. Today, during your visit to the doctor's office, you discovered that you are pregnant. What would you do?

Situation 2

This is the year that you and your spouse had planned to have your first child. Today your wife was offered a promotion on her job that would require a great deal of overtime. Previously, she had planned to stop working for a few years to stay home with the new baby. However, an offer like this doesn't come often. What would you do?

Situation 3

This year you and your husband have planned to celebrate your fifth anniversary (which is this weekend) in Las Vegas. You have made plans for a friend to keep your two-year-old child while you and your husband are away. Today is Thursday and you just found out that your child has the measles. Your friend also has a two-year-old child. (Your child was to stay at your friend's house.) What would you do? Why?

MAJOR COMPETENCY: The student can utilize the decision-making process in determining if and when to become a parent.

Subcompetencies	Possible Generalizations
The student can---	
---select procedures for implementing short- and long-term plans to reach parenting goals.	3. As unexpected events or opportunities may cause one to alter plans for achievement of goals, plans need to be flexible...continued.

Learning Activities	Resources
Situation 4 You have finally saved enough money to replace your three-year-old coat with a new one. Just before you leave to go shopping to catch the sales, your seven-year-old child comes home from school in tears. He lost his coat and mittens. What would you do? Situation 5 Erica and Van are both established in their careers and have been married five years. They have been trying to have a baby for two years but they have not been successful. Erica's doctor has just informed her that she cannot conceive a child. Suggest alternatives for the couple to consider since they both really like children and want to parent.	

MAJOR COMPETENCY: The student can utilize the decision-making process in determining if and when to become a parent.

Subcompetencies	Possible Generalizations
The student can---	
---analyze one's own feelings about becoming a parent.	1. Since the role of the parent is highly demanding and one that cannot be revoked, it is important for a person to clearly analyze his/her feelings about becoming a parent.
	2. One's feelings about becoming a parent may be influenced by societal values, familial wishes, and peer pressure.

Learning Activities	Resources
1.1 Have each student read and react to the rating scale "My Feelings About Becoming a Parent" (Appendix B-9). Encourage students to state reasons for their responses to the items on the rating scale in a class discussion.	
1.2 Assign pp. 4-11 in <u>School-Age Parenthood</u>. Discuss in class.	Nye, F. <u>School-Age Parenthood</u>. 1978.
2.1 Ask students to list 5 reasons for having a family. Discuss in class to determine if the reasons listed might be influenced by personal feelings, family wishes, peer pressure, or societal conditions.	
2.2 Have each student read "Factors That Influence My Decision to Parent" (Appendix B-10). Discuss students' reponse to the relative importance of each item and compare to the reasons listed in 2.1.	
2.3 Ask for a volunteer group of students to role play the following situation: A teenage couple, high school sophomores, has been dating for seven months. During the girl's yearly checkup she discovers she is pregnant. The characters for the role play are the teenage couple, friends of the couple, parents of each teenager, and others suggested by the class. Instruct students to illustrate in the role play possible reactions each character might have upon learning of the pregnancy.	

MAJOR COMPETENCY: The student can utilize the decision-making process in determining if and when to become a parent.

Subcompetencies	Possible Generalizations
The student can---	
---analyze one's own feelings about becoming a parent.	2. One's feelings about becoming a parent may be influenced by societal values, familial wishes, and peer pressure...continued.

Learning Activities	Resources
Summarize the role play by encouraging the characters in the play and other students to: a. Suggest alternatives that could be considered in solving the problem, i.e., abortion, adoption, marriage, non-marriage with grandparents raising the child. b. Discuss how each alternative would affect the teenage couple, their parents, their peers, their child (if no abortion).	
2.4 Collect current articles from newspapers, journals, magazines, pamphlets, books, related to the above topics for students to use. Place in a reading corner in the classroom.	
(or)	
Have students read "I Refused to Give Up My Baby." Discuss following topics: a. Reaction of girl b. Reaction of parents c. Reaction of society d. Loneliness of girl e. Financial problems f. Alternatives	David, L. "I Refused to Give Up My Baby." *Seventeen*. June 1977, pp. 162-63, 183, 194.

MAJOR COMPETENCY: The student can utilize the decision-making process in determining if and when to become a parent.

Subcompetencies	Possible Generalizations
The student can---	
---analyze one's own ability to make decisions regarding parenthood.	1. The ability to make decisions is influenced by the amount of practice one has had.
	2. One's ability to make decisions is largely dependent on the amount and kind of available information.

Learning Activities	Resources
1.1 Ask students to list kinds of decisions they made as a sixth grader. Compare this with decisions they are making now. Discuss: ----Have the number of decisions you make increased? --- Have the types of decisions you make changed? --- Why? --- What steps did(do) you follow in arriving at a decision? As a sixth grader? At present time?	
1.2 Assign students to investigate in small groups --- Possible outcomes --- Risks of making decisions based upon: --- Impulse --- Trial and error --- Past experience --- Results of past decisions ---yours ---your friends --- Feelings (values?) --- Facts (goals?) Prepare an illustration of each technique based upon personal experience. Discuss group reports.	Paolucci,B.,Faiola,T.,& Thompson,P. <u>Personal Perspectives</u>. 1978. Chapters 1-4.
2.1 Review with students the decision-making process, using a variety of resources, filmstrips, texts, transparencies. (or) Apply the decision-making process to case studies to practice skills in using the process.	Filmstrip: <u>Decision Making Skills</u>. Guidance Associates. <u>Rational Decision Making Process</u>. 3-M Transparencies. <u>Decisions and Outcomes</u>. Home Economics School Service.

MAJOR COMPETENCY: The student can utilize the decision-making process in determining if and when to become a parent.

Subcompetencies	Possible Generalizations
The student can---	
---analyze one's own ability to make decisions regarding parenthood.	2. One's ability to make decisions is largely dependent on the amount and kind of available information ...continued.
	3. Feelings and emotions affect one's ability to make decisions regarding parenthood.

Learning Activities	Resources
2.2 Divide class into groups. Ask each group, using the decision-making process, to resolve a case study involving making a decision in regard to parenting. Report to class and discuss in terms of alternatives, outcomes, risks, information needed, etc. Examples: ● a. Sonja and Jim are high school seniors. Sonja is pregnant. Both want to continue their education, Jim at the university and Sonja at a technical school. Sonja is working 12 hours a week at the bakery, Jim works 18 hours a week at a service station. Help them make a decision in regard to parenting. Examples of possible alternatives for discussion: ---Abortion vs. having child ---Marriage vs. nonmarriage ---Parents caring for child vs. grandparents caring for child b. Ned and Susan have been married two years. Ned is assistant manager of a local food store and Susan has just been promoted to assistant bookkeeper at a car agency. Susan's parents want grandchildren. Help Susan and Ned make a decision in regard to parenting.	
3.1 Brainstorm in class: Why may feelings and emotions be factors in decisions regarding parenthood? Discuss: How do(can) you keep feelings and emotions in perspective when making personal decisions?	Paolucci,B., Faiola,T., & Thompson,P. <u>Personal Perspectives</u>. 1978. Chapters 1-4. "Teenage Pregnancy." <u>Co-ed</u>, May 1978.

MAJOR COMPETENCY: The student can utilize the decision-making process in determining if and when to become a parent.

Subcompetencies	Possible Generalizations
The student can---	
---analyze one's own ability to make decisions regarding parenthood.	3. Feelings and emotions affect one's ability to make decisions regarding parenthood...continued.

Learning Activities	Resources
Ask students to search references for more information.	"Right Now." McCalls Magazine, July 1978, pp. 45-52.
3.2 Show film You Can't Mean Not Ever.	Whelan, E.M. A Baby? Maybe. 1975.
Ask students to watch for examples of how feelings and emotions may affect decisions regarding parenting. Discuss as a group after watching film.	Film: You Can't Mean Not Ever. University of Minn. 1977.
3.3 Assign individual discussion papers:	
What experience and information do I have that will help me make a decision regarding parenting?	

MAJOR COMPETENCY: The student can utilize the decision-making process in determining if and when to become a parent.

Subcompetencies	Possible Generalizations
The student can---	
---accept responsibility for one's own decisions regarding parenthood.	1. Developing a sense of responsibility implies acceptance of personal decisions and a range of consequences.

Learning Activities	Resources
1.1 Show the film <u>Personal Commitment--Where Do You Stand?</u> Discuss: --- What does a sense of responsibility mean to you? --- How can you develop a sense of responsibility for your decisions? --- How have you reacted when the consequences of your decisions have not turned out the way you would have liked? --- What kinds of personal decisions have you had difficulty accepting responsibility for?	Film: <u>Personal Commitment--Where Do You Stand?</u> Guidance Associates.
1.2 Collect pictures of small groups of individuals. Have these pictures show individuals at different ages and stages of life. Examples might be a woman (20-25) with a baby, a teenage couple, a man (30-35) with an elementary school child, an elderly person with a teenager. Divide the class into small groups of students. Give each group a picture and a copy of the chart "Decisions and Responsibility" (Appendix B-11). Have the groups discuss the following questions and summarize on the chart: --- What is happening in the picture? --- What kinds of decisions might each individual in the picture have to make? --- What are some possible consequences of these decisions? --- How do you think the individuals in the pictures would react to these consequences? --- Who is responsible for the decisions made by the individuals?	

MAJOR COMPETENCY: The student can utilize the decision-making process in determining if and when to become a parent.

Subcompetencies	Possible Generalizations
The student can---	
---accept responsibility for one's own decisions regarding parenthood.	1. Developing a sense of responsibility implies acceptance of personal decisions and a range of consequences... continued.
	2. The decision to parent often involves accepting responsibilities not anticipated at the time the decision was made.

Learning Activities	Resources
Share group reports. Compare and contrast the types of decisions, consequences, reactions and responsibilities based on the age of the individual pictured and the role each individual was playing.	
1.3 Have students read "Teenage Pregnancy: ● Whose Fault?" or develop a case study based on the article. Discuss: --- Do young men generally think it is their responsibility to use birth control? --- How will a responsible young man act before and during a sexual relationship? A responsible young woman? --- Who will be responsible for caring for the child of teenage parents? Mother? Father? Grandparents?	Wax, J. "Teenage Pregnancy: Whose Fault?" <u>Seventeen</u>. Oct. 1978, pp. 132, 172-73.
2.1 Have students read "A Time to Choose." ● Discuss: --- What decisions did Barbara not anticipate having to make when she and Mike decided to become sexually active? When they decided to have and raise a child? --- How did Barbara feel when she was visiting her former classmates? How do you think Mike is feeling now? --- What did the baby's choking help Barbara to realize? --- How do you think you would react if you were in Barbara's place now? If you had a child later?	Exter, M. "A Time to Choose." <u>Coed</u>. April 1978, pp. 68-70, 78.

MAJOR COMPETENCY: The student can utilize the decision-making process in determining if and when to become a parent.

Subcompetencies	Possible Generalizations
The student can---	
---accept responsibility for one's own decisions regarding parenthood.	2. The decision to parent often involves accepting responsibilities not anticipated at the time the decision was made...continued.

Learning Activities	Resources
2.2 Have resource person(s) come to class and ☐ speak on accepting parental responsibilities. These resource individuals should be parents of exceptional children (i.e., physically handicapped, mentally handicapped, talented or gifted). Ask the individual(s) to talk about the responsibilities they expected to accept as a parent and the additional responsibilities because they are parents of exceptional children. How have they reacted to these additional responsibilities? What community resources are available to help them?	

APPENDIX A

MAJOR COMPETENCY: The student can appraise the variety of responsibilities involved in being a parent.

PATTERNS OF GROWTH*

ASSIGNMENT: Read references to find information on the patterns of growth in children and children's needs, both in the four basic areas: emotional, social, intellectual, and physical. Make brief notes in the appropriate block.

AREAS	PATTERNS OF GROWTH	CHILDREN'S NEEDS
EMOTIONAL		
SOCIAL		
INTELLECTUAL		
PHYSICAL size		
motor		

*Developed by Parent Education Project Staff, Iowa State University, 1979.

FATHERS, MOTHERS, AND OTHERS*

In an attempt to discover who has served parenting roles in your life, consider the following questions:

WHO TAUGHT YOU TO RIDE A BIKE?

WHO TAUGHT YOU TO DO YOUR FAVORITE HOBBY?

WHERE DID YOU FIRST LEARN TO READ? FROM WHOM?

FROM WHOM DID YOU FIRST LEARN ABOUT SEX?

WHERE DID YOU LEARN TO PLAY YOUR FAVORITE GAME? FROM WHOM?

WHO HELPED YOU UNDERSTAND YOUR RELIGIOUS BELIEFS?

WHO DO YOU GO TO WHEN YOU NEED SOMEONE TO LISTEN?

---

*Adapted from: _Parenting: Fathers, Mothers, and Others_. J. C. Penney Co., 1975.

PARTS PEOPLE PLAY*

We all have ideas about what mothers and fathers should be or do. What words do YOU associate with these roles?

1. Under the column heading marked "role of father" and "role of mother" place an X if the word in your opinion describes that role.

2. Choose one person other than your mother and father who has parented you. Place an X in the column "role of other parent" beside the words that best describe that person.

3. In the last column, "my parenting role," place an X beside the word that describes yourself when you are parenting others.

4. Review your list and circle the words you marked in at least three categories. What is basic in your definition of parenting?

5. Write a definition of parenting.

role of mother	role of father	role of other parent	my parenting role	
				understanding
				loving
				helping
				caring
				punishing
				kind
				cheerful
				sharing
				angry
				carefree
				responsible
				traditional
				creative
				fair
				perceptive
				sensitive
				others

---

*Adapted from: Parenting: Mothers, Fathers, and Others. J. C. Penney, 1975.

CHILDREN LEARN WHAT THEY LIVE*

IF CHILDREN LIVE WITH
CRITICISM,
THEY LEARN TO CONDEMN.

IF CHILDREN LIVE WITH
HOSTILITY,
THEY LEARN TO FIGHT.

IF CHILDREN LIVE WITH
RIDICULE,
THEY LEARN TO BE SHY.

IF CHILDREN LIVE WITH
SHAME,
THEY LEARN TO FEEL GUILTY.

IF CHILDREN LIVE WITH
TOLERANCE,
THEY LEARN TO BE PATIENT.

IF CHILDREN LIVE WITH
ENCOURAGEMENT,
THEY LEARN CONFIDENCE.

IF CHILDREN LIVE WITH
PRAISE,
THEY LEARN TO APPRECIATE.

IF CHILDREN LIVE WITH
FAIRNESS,
THEY LEARN JUSTICE.

IF CHILDREN LIVE WITH
SECURITY,
THEY LEARN TO HAVE FAITH.

IF CHILDREN LIVE WITH
APPROVAL,
THEY LEARN TO LIKE THEMSELVES.

IF CHILDREN LIVE WITH
ACCEPTANCE AND FRIENDSHIP,
THEY LEARN TO FIND LOVE IN
THE WORLD.

---

*Adapted from Dorothy Law Nolte.

DEVELOPMENTAL STAGES FOR ADULTS

Adults will move through the developmental stages at various rates. Those stages suggested will not be alike for all.

Stage of Life	Tasks To Be Accomplished
Establishing Identity 17-21	Leave family Begin independent living Explore career possibilities Commence work Cultivate peer relationships Make decisions about sexual activity Establish residence Sharpen management skills Develop decision-making skills Cope with change
Young Adulthood 22-30	Choose a life style (marriage vs. nonmarriage) Parent (vs. not to parent) Begin career escalation Explore possible community contribution Establish home Achieve independence Scrutinize social involvements Develop decision-making skills Cope with change
Maturity 30-40	Prioritize goals Advance in career Reevaluate personal relationships Guide developing children Utilize decision-making skills Cope with change
Established Middle Years 40-50	Examine personal values Solidify career goals Promote emotional independence of children Manage budgetary responsibilities: school for children, aid to parents Achieve social and civic responsibility Contemplate (or adjust to) single living Cope with change
Late Maturity 50-60	Accept career commitment/attainment Release children Contribute actively to selected (personal choice) civic activities Care for aging parents Deepen social involvement Plan use of and enjoy leisure time Cope with change

Developmental Stages*- continued

Stage of Life	Tasks To Be Accomplished
Planning for Retirement 60-65 or 60-70	Prepare for retirement Adapt to increased medical problems Enjoy long-standing personal relationships Explore avocational interests Accept inevitability of death--mate, parents, friends, children Solve problems Cope with change
Retirement 65+ or 70+	Cease paid employment Plan for utilization of financial resources Increase attention to personal health care Share increased time with spouse or Adjust to single living Explore outlets for creative energy/leisure time Accept death Solve problems Cope with change

*Developed by Parent Education Project Staff, Iowa State University, 1979.

YOUR BUDGET - - - CAN YOU AFFORD A CHILD?*

NAME________________

MONTHLY INCOME (Teacher specifies)

SPOUSE'S MONTHLY INCOME (Teacher specifies)

UNEARNED INCOME - Dividends, interests, etc. (Teacher specifies)

MONTHLY EXPENSES:

Taxes and social security (¼) ________________

Rent or house payment ________________

House upkeep ________________

Phone ________________

Electricity ________________

Gas ________________

Water ________________

Home furnishings ________________

Credit payments ________________

Car payment ________________

Car repairs ________________

Life insurance ________________

Health insurance ________________

Car insurance ________________

Clothes ________________

Food ________________

Entertainment ________________

Gasoline ________________

Gifts ________________

Savings ________________

Debts ________________

Other (list) ________________

TOTAL MONTHLY INCOME ________________ TOTAL MONTHLY EXPENSES ________________

(Attach a newspaper ad describing an apartment or house.)

*Developed by Parent Education Project Staff, Iowa State University, 1979.

APPENDIX B

MAJOR COMPETENCY: The student can use the decision-making process in determining if and when to become a parent.

WHAT DO YOU THINK*

Respond to the following statements by placing a check (✓) in the appropriate column: SA (strongly agree), A (agree), D (disagree) and SD (strongly disagree).

	SA	A	D	SD
1. Children can be raised just as successfully by one person as by a couple.	____	____	____	____
2. Large families are better than small families for children.	____	____	____	____
3. I would want to have a child even if I did not marry.	____	____	____	____
4. Raising adopted children is different from raising your own children.	____	____	____	____
5. Women and men **can** be equally good parents.	____	____	____	____
6. Children with both parents in the home usually are happier than children with divorced parents.	____	____	____	____

*Developed by Parent Education Project Staff, Iowa State University, 1979.

I was going pretty steady with Jay, and sometimes I worried a little about getting pregnant. But I really didn't believe I would, so I didn't think about it much. Then I missed two periods. After the second miss, I thought I'd better tell *somebody*—but I didn't want to worry my boyfriend Jay, and I was scared to tell my mother. Finally I told Jay, and he *did* worry—he said I'd better go see a doctor right away. Well, I sure didn't want to see the doctor Ma goes to—and I didn't want to go to the school clinic. So I went to the Family Health Clinic at the hospital—I'd seen pregnant girls going there. Jay helped me get the courage to go, and I sure was nervous!

You know what? They acted okay. I met a doctor there, a woman doctor. I really could talk to her. She checked me over, said I was in fine shape. Then she asked, did I have any plans for the baby? Like keeping it, or having it adopted. I hadn't thought about what to do after the baby came. I was too busy worrying about what Ma would say. Dr. Rose said I had a lot of time to decide. Right now, she'd show me how to take care of myself and the baby. And she and the other people there would help me with Ma, too.

Well, just as I knew, Ma blew her top! But it was easier for us both having Dr. Rose there. Ma even calmed down enough to help me with my school plans, and she said she was going to make sure I eat right! And Jay's going to help support the baby.

Right now, I'm feeling pretty good. I'm feeling a little sick in the morning, but Dr. Rose says that will stop. My breasts are swollen and tender, and I get tired more often than before. I've cut out eating junk food, and I've quit smoking. I'm still in school, and I've got time to think about the future. The important thing right now is looking after that little baby growing inside me—and I'm doing just that!

Inside Your Body, Inside Your Head. National Foundation--March of Dimes, 1978.

PARENTING QUESTIONNAIRE*

The purpose of this questionnaire is to find out how having children affects on parents. Please interview five adults, preferably of different ages, with different aged children, different numbers of children, and/or different life styles. Ask them to respond to these questions without placing their names on the questionnaire. After you have interviewed all the adults, analyze the results according to the questions at the end of the questionnaire.

1. Did you make a conscious decision to have your first child?
   If so, what made you think you were ready for children?
   If not, do you feel you were ready for children?
   Why or why not?
2. Why did you want to have children?
3. What physical changes did your first child make in your life?
4. What economic changes did your first child make in your life?
5. What emotional changes did having a child make in your life?
6. What role changes occurred between the parents after the first child was born?
7. What do you wish you had known before having children?
8. What support could have helped you cope with having and rearing children?
9. What additional changes were made in your life with the addition of other children?
10. Would you choose to have children again if you had it to do over? Why or why not?
11. What have you liked best about being a parent?
12. What has been most difficult about being a parent?
13. What other comments would you like to make?

Students: Analyze all your questionnaires for:

a. Satisfaction with parenthood,
b. Reasons for having children,
c. Effects of children on life styles
d. What to be prepared for when having children.

---

*<u>Tips and Topics</u>, Vol. XVIII, No. 3, Spring 1978, p. 6.

Baby Bill of Rights

TALK TO ME,
Sing, hum, babble, or even read the funnies to me! I don't know exactly what you're saying, but I need to hear you. And I do know what you mean, even if I may not know words. Like your voice tones mean, "I love you." Or when you yell, I hear, "You're a pest!" Unless you communicate with me, how can I learn? I learn from you.

HOLD ME.
Everything is so big and new to me. I don't understand where I am. Or who I am. And I get scared. But when you hold me, I feel better. Your warmth warms me. Your breath and heartbeat make me feel I belong. Belong here. Belong to you.

ANSWER MY CRY.
I don't cry to get you upset. Or to get you mad. I cry because I can't tell you how I feel any other way. Maybe I'm cold...or wet...or hungry...or scared and lonely. Answer my cries. You'll soon know what each one means. You won't spoil me. You'll help me to be a better baby—and to make you happier, too.

LOVE ME.
Like me. Love me just as I am. Don't expect me to do what I can't do. Like being toilet-trained. My muscles aren't ready yet. I know I'm messy. But I'm growing. Overlook my baby weaknesses. You're the most important person in my world. I can't make it without you. So get to know me. Have fun with me. And love me—just as I am.

Inside Your Body, Inside Your Head. National Foundation--March of Dimes, 1978.

STRATEGY 4--LEARNING CENTERS*

"School-Age Parenthood"

Four objectives for setting up learning centers on school-age parenthood are presented. Activities that might be used to accomplish Objective A are included:

Objective A	The student will identify effects of school-age parenthood on babies, mothers, fathers, grandparents and others.
Objective B	The student will analyze decisions teenagers can make concerning parenthood.
Objective C	The student will discuss how teenagers influence their peers in encouraging or preventing school-age parenthood.
Objective D	The students will analyze the role parents can play in preventing school-age parenthood.

LEARNING CENTER A--GROUP DIRECTIONS AND ACTIVITIES

MEMBERS: ____________________ ____________________

____________________ ____________________

ACTIVITY #1:

In the center of your table are copies of the publication "School-Age Parenthood." Each student take a copy of the publication and Activity Sheet A. Follow the directions on the activity sheet.

ACTIVITY #2:

After all the members of your group have finished Activity Sheet A, have one member of your group read the instructions on Activity Sheet B. Follow the directions on Activity Sheet B and complete the activity as a group. Hand in all completed worksheets to be check by your teacher.

ACTIVITY #3:

When your group has finished Activity Sheet B, have each individual respond to the questions on Activity Sheet C. As a group compare your answers. Read pages 9-11. Go back to the questions and star those which are true based on the reading.

ACTIVITY #4:

As a group, summarize what you have learned about the effects of school-age parenthood. Include the following: effects on babies, mothers, fathers, grandparents, and others. A good way to start would be for each group member to tell one thing he/she has learned. Write your statements in the space below.

Hand in all materials to the teacher.

---

*Schultz, J. Classroom Strategies for Teaching Parenting. Iowa Home Economics Teachers' Conference, 1978.

NAME________________________

ACTIVITY SHEET A

Read pages 2-4 on "Effects on Babies." List the four major effects of school-age parenthood on babies. Give one fact presented in the reading which supports that school-age parenthood has this effect on babies.

EFFECT	FACT
1. ________________________	________________________
2. ________________________	________________________
3. ________________________	________________________
4. ________________________	________________________

Group Members:________________________

____

____

____

ACTIVITY SHEET B

Divide the group in half. Have one half read pages 4-7 and the other half read pages 7-8. After all of the group have finished the reading, have one member read the case study aloud. Have one member record the answers to the questions on the activity sheet.

CASE STUDY: Susan and Bill are seniors in high school. They have been going steady for two years. They have been having intercourse and have not been using any contraceptive device. What are some of the consequences a pregnancy now could have on Susan? On Bill?

NAME______________________________

ACTIVITY SHEET C

Circle A if you agree with the statement and D if you disagree with the statement.

A D 1. School-age mothers are able to support themselves and their babies.

A D 2. Parents of school-age mothers often have to take care of the babies.

A D 3. A large number of school-age mothers will end up on welfare.

A D 4. A school-age mother who marries the baby's father is better able to provide for the baby.

A D 5. School-age parenthood affects everyone.

Teen parenthood: A web of heartaches

By FRANCES CRAIG
Register Staff Writer

"One of the main difficulties of being a teen-ager is sex, at once a great discovery, a great mess, a great pleasure and an all around great muddle .... " — Daniel Callahan in "11 Million Teen-agers," published by the Alan Guttmacher Institute.

One of the most troubling aspects of the teen-ager's "muddle" about sex is how many other persons can be pained by it when it results in pregnancy or birth.

Besides a girl and her baby, there are a father (probably a teen-ager, too) and two sets of grandparents.

In an ever widening pebble-in-the-pool effect, others are affected, too — ultimately taxpayers in many cases.

Consider these facts:

- Last year, 6,298 girls between the ages of 10 and 19 gave birth in Iowa. They were responsible for more than 15 percent of all the babies born to all mothers, all ages.
- About one-third were unmarried, compared with about one-fourth five years ago.
- The total for teen-age births was up 90 from the year before. There are indications that the figure for 1978 will be up again.
- Nationally, one in 10 teen-age girls becomes pregnant each year.

Commenting on the spiraling trend of teen-age parenthood, Joseph Califano Jr., secretary of the U.S. Department of Health, Education and Welfare (HEW), said last spring that teen-age parents are caught in a "form of bondage."

It is a complex bondage with often-unexpected chains. For example, teen-age parents are more likely to be burdened with defective babies, medical studies show, partly because the mothers have not reached full biological maturity and partly because they often have poorer diets and inadequate medical care.

Perhaps the most common "bondage" is one of adulthood, assumed too early.

The teen mother

Mary is a Des Moines teen-ager who knows what Califano means by "bondage."

She loves her 8-month-old son and is grateful that he is flawless and beautiful, but Mary says, "It's a struggle taking care of two people and not having any teen-age life."

She was 16 and a junior at North High School when she became pregnant. Wedded to Tom, 19, after the discovery, she has had an off-again, on-again marriage.

Mary says she had gone with Tom for three years, and they had had sexual relations two years without precautions before she became pregnant.

"I was kind of nervous at first, but then nothing happened. Anyway, I thought you'd have to go to a doctor to get birth control, and he'd tell your parents. Somebody should tell kids to go to Planned Parenthood; they'll keep it confidential — I know that now."

When Mary told her parents about her predicament, they were "very, very upset, but not angry." She remembers their saying, "We always think this happens to the neighbors' kids, not our own."

An abortion was considered and rejected.

Although she and Tom had decided they could marry and handle the situation themselves, her parents were not so sure. "One of Mom's biggest worries was about my health," Mary says.

Her mother's worries were justified. The death rate from complications of pregnancy and childbirth is 13 percent greater for 15- to 19-year-olds than for women in their early 20s — 60 per-cent greater for teen-agers 14 and under.

"We thought about my having the baby and putting it up for adoption. My mother leaned toward that — then less so after we married," Mary says.

Finances also had worried her parents, owners of a small business in which both work. Mary says the main thing that reassured them it was all right to get married was that Tom had completed high school and a year's training at an area college as a welder.

Also, Mary thought she had a good grasp on finances. "My folks always discussed how much things cost with us kids; I had helped grocery shop and handled my own clothes-buying."

Even so, the birth went easier than the finances later.

Their 8½-pound son was born with only moderate difficulty at Broadlawns Polk County Hospital at a cost of $525, a sum determined by her husband's income.

Unable to find work as a welder, he was employed by a chemical company, with take-home pay of $115 per week.

With painful budgeting, she says they paid off the medical bill. Monthly rent was $180 for their small apartment. There never was money enough for groceries and anything extra ("not even a hamburger at McDonald's").

Tensions built up when he began bringing home friends for dinner, a stab at sociability that *really* shot the budget.

Money hassles finally resulted in a big blow-up, and they separated when the baby was five months old. She filed for dissolution and went to live with her parents.

Before and after the birth, Mary had continued her education at Temple School of Booth Services, a day-time school for young married and unmarried mothers, underwritten by the Des Moines Public Schools.

Welfare checks

After the separation, her parents helped find a small apartment near Temple and bought a stroller for her to transport her baby to the nursery at the school. He still attends with 40 or more tots each school day.

She filed for Aid to Dependent Children (ADC). For three months, she received $275 monthly plus $100 in food stamps, hating every check. "I wasn't raised to accept welfare," she says.

In recent weeks, she and Tom have been back together and she is off welfare. Dissolution proceedings have been dropped. He has found a welding job paying $210 weekly and he has a second job, painting houses.

Education for her was and is important: "Ever since sixth grade, I've wanted to be a court reporter," she says. Toward that end, her father is working out plans to finance her enrollment at a business college.

Things are working out, but it isn't always easy. "I love my baby and try to be a good mother, but there's a lot I don't know," Mary says. "I read everything I can on child raising .... But sometimes I get very frustrated and depressed."

It would be easy for a teen-age parent to be a child abuser, Mary says. Her baby is teething now and cries a lot: "Sometimes I have to just put him down and shut the door and just not let myself get angry."

Among some 20 teen-age mothers with whom she associates, Mary says she knows two who have had their babies removed by the courts because of abuse and neglect — "and I know about five others who ought to have them taken away."

Was it a wise and realistic decision for her to keep her son?

Mary looks away for a long time while the interviewer studies the childish-appearing teenager, recalling a doctor's comment from a previous interview. He said the immature mother never grows any taller after she has completed pregnancy; long bone-ends close during the process.

Mary answers at last. "Of course, I'm glad I have him. But many times, I've thought he would be better off growing up somewhere else.

"Just yesterday, I got together with some girls I knew in junior high, and I thought. they're having so much fun. Why am I not there?"

When was the last big dance she attended? "It was in junior high," says Mary. "I went to the Snow Queen Dance all three years I was in junior high — with dates."

The teen father

Being born on "the right side of the tracks" is no guarantee of easier teen-age parenthood — or so the experience of 30-year-old Scott would indicate as he looks back over a 13-year haul.

He and his girlfriend came from what usually are called "substantial" families. They were juniors at Roosevelt High School in Des Moines when she became pregnant.

Although they considered it an accident at the time, Scott now considers the pregnancy "unconsciously on-purpose."

"I think it was a feeling of rebellion. For both of us, it was a way out of our parents' houses," he says.

His parents were strict with high expectations of their children. Former schoolmates and teachers remember him as one of the brightest boys in his class.

Her parents had high expectations, too, including a well-educated son-in-law who would support their daughter in good style.

When the youngsters learned of her pregnancy, they were married secretly in Missouri. They found an apartment and planned to announce the marriage in a month, but her mother found out earlier, and he says, "All hell broke loose."

Her mother wanted an abortion, an annulment, or at least for Bonnie to go away and have the baby, Scott relates. "That left us no choice except to stay married. The most bull-headed man I know is my father — and I'm like him, I guess."

His own parents were urging him to look at it reasonably, he says, "but we punched the ticket and moved to the apartment."

Rocky relationship

It was a disaster, he says. "We were the only kids our age married, so everybody wanted to party and drink at our apartment."

Scott quit school and found a job in a lumber yard. "I had to be there at 6 a.m., and I would step over our friends' bodies as I got ready for work," he says.

A month later, they moved to his parents' house — another disaster. He says they both were too immature to accommodate to each other's parents.

Back in an apartment, Bonnie struggled with housework and Scott came home at the end of 12-hour working days. His earnings were $1.20 an hour.

Their first son was born, now 12, and then a second, 9, (both handsome and healthy). In between, there were separations, and Bonnie filed twice for divorce before she pursued the action to a bitter finish. Both were 21.

By then, he says, "the marriage had deteriorated into a non-support, non-sexual relationship." He had developed drinking and drug habits

"I was grossly irresponsible," he says.

By then, however, he was making good money (sometimes $2,000 per month) selling crockeryware to young working women and training other glib young salesmen in the art. However, "I blew that, too, because of my immaturity and unreliability."

Although Scott had dropped out of school, Bonnie had completed her schooling through night school, a year after the rest of her class.

Periodically, Scott made stabs at getting his diploma from Roosevelt. Finally, in 1969 (when he was 21), he visited a Des Moines school board member, wound up in a long conversation amounting to a kind of oral exam — and received his diploma six months later in the mail, dated 1966.

After the divorce, Scott collected on loans he had made to crockeryware sales staff members, enabling him to pay child support dictated by the courts. He has continued to pay child support, now set at $50 per week.

Delayed adolescence

He lived at home for a year in something like delayed adolescence, then went to work in his father's office supply company where he currently is a salesman. He has come to terms with the idea of working for his father: "Sometimes I think, here I am 30 and working for my dad. But I've pretty well resolved that; I tell myself no one else could work for him."

He went through a series of lovers and recently remarried: "Once I said I never would marry again. Now, it sticks in my craw to say it, but I believe marriage is necessary."

With obvious satisfaction, he relates that he and Bonnie are good friends, "almost like a brother and sister," and he feels good about his relationship with his sons. Nine months ago, he completed an alcoholic treatment program and joined Alcoholics Anonymous. "I should have done it long ago," he says.

Did he make a realistic decision in that spring of 1965 when he and Bonnie decided to keep their baby?

Scott contemplates the question: "That's a tough one ...."

"No, I guess it wasn't a realistic decision," he says. "A realist would have waited until he was grown up himself before he had children. It might be 30, and it might be never."

Still, he says he came out of their teen-age marriage better than most.

"Bonnie and I paid the full emotional cost in going through the thing. Now, we're both close to our

Teens' parents

One significant statistic concerning teen-age parenthood is that at least 85 percent of Iowa's unwed mothers keep their babies.

It is too soon to know what the effects will be: The jury will consist of the "kept" children themselves, and the panel will be out for a time.

Only one thing is clear: "Extended family" has come to have new meanings, particularly for maternal grandparents.

Shirley Leonard, school social worker at Temple School, says it is a rare instance where a grandmother is not greatly involved in the lives of a "keeping" mother and baby.

Often the grandmother quits a job or postpones her plans for a pleasant "empty nest" in order to help.

A Connecticut study showed that of single mothers continuing in school, 52 percent left their babies with their mothers. Two years later, of those still in school, two-thirds were leaving their babies with their mothers.

Eighty-one percent of the grandparents were giving their daughters financial help at the outset, and two years later, 51 percent still were helping.

Many tears

Mrs. H is one Des Moines grandmother involved in the "keeping" trend. Her grandson was born in 1975 to her unmarried 14-year-old daughter.

Mrs. H says she can't remember how she learned her daughter was pregnant, but that "believe me, there were plenty of tears at the time."

The baby's father, also a teen-ager, never figured in the planning, she says; he simply "faded out."

Although Mrs. H is separated from

her husband, he contributes to the support of his three daughters and takes an active interest in them. It was a family decision to keep the baby.

Mrs. H's circumstances require that she work part time and this has meant juggling schedules in order to baby-sit with the child while her daughter works as a clerk-typist. She no longer has access to the nursery at Temple School.

Mrs. H and administrators at Temple consider the young woman a real success story: With determination, she continued her schooling at Temple after leaving junior high school and she graduated a year early from high school, relates Mrs. H.

During the three years she was in school, the girl was on ADC, receiving an average of $145 per month, says the grandmother. Now, she is self-supporting.

But, could she manage without her mother and other relatives baby sitting? "Oh, no. There's no way!" says Mrs. H.

She thinks the situation has worked out better than most; for one thing, her grandson "knows who his mother is." That's not the case with some she knows in similar situations, she says.

The daughter dates now and Mrs. H thinks she eventually will marry.

"It certainly has changed my life," says the grandmother. "I don't always feel cut out to look after a baby at my age (in her 50s). You look forward to the time you will relax and have things the way you want.

"I have an awfully sweet grandchild, but it's just not the same as when they come to visit."

Des Moines Sunday Register
November 12, 1978

Is my lifestyle conducive to parenting?

1. Would a child interfere with my educational plans? Would I have the energy to go to school and raise a child at the same time?
2. Would a child restrict my individual growth and development?
3. Could I handle children and a career well? Am I tired when I come home from work or do I have lots of energy left?
4. Does my job or my partner's job require a lot of traveling?
5. Am I financially able to support a child? Am I prepared to spend almost $100 a week to rear my child to age 18? or over $80,000, not including one partner's income loss if he/she would choose to remain at home?
6. Do I live in a neighborhood conducive to raising a child? Would I be willing to move?
7. Would I be willing to give up the freedom to do what I want to do, when I want to do it?
8. Would I be willing to restrict my social life? Would I miss lost leisure time and privacy?
9. Would my partner and I be prepared to spend more time at home? Would we have enough time to spend with a child?
10. Would I be willing to devote a great part of my life, at **least** 18 years, to being responsible for a child? and spend my entire life being concerned about my child's welfare?
11. Would I be prepared to be a single parent if my partner left or died?

Good luck in making your decision, and good wishes for a happy and fulfilled future.

This paper was prepared by Carole Goldman, Executive Director of the National Organization for Non-Parents, in cooperation with Elizabeth K. Canfield, Health and Family Planning Counselor, University of Southern California; Dr. Robert E. Gould, Professor of Psychiatry, New York Medical College; and Dr. Burleigh Seaver, Research Associate, Pennsylvania State University Institute for Research on Human Resources.

Additional copies of "AM I PARENT MATERIAL?" are available from the National Organization for Non-Parents, 806 Reisterstown Road, Baltimore, Md. 21208.
1-9, 6c each; 10-99, 5c each; 100 or more 4c each

AM I PARENT MATERIAL?:

A thoughtful questionnaire about the most important decision I'll ever make.

These questions are posed to you as you consider the most important decision you will ever make—whether or not to have a child. The decision to have a child is one that you will live with for the rest of your life. The responsibility of a new life is awesome. These questions are designed to raise ideas that you may not have otherwise considered. There are no "right" answers and no "grades". You must decide for yourself what your answers reveal about your aptitude for parenthood.

You **do** have a choice. Exercise that choice with knowledge and careful thought. And then do what seems right for you.

to raise a child?

1. Do I like children? Have I had enough experiences with babies? toddlers? teenagers?
2. Do I enjoy teaching others?
3. Do I communicate easily with others?
4. Do I have enough love to give a child? Can I express affection easily?
5. Would I have the patience to raise a child? Can I tolerate noise and confusion? Can I deal with disrupted schedules?
6. How do I handle anger? Would I abuse my child if I lost my temper?
7. What do I know about discipline and freedom? about setting limits and giving space? Would I be too strict? too lenient? Am I a perfectionist? How do I deal with change?
8. Do I know my own values and goals yet? Could I help my child develop constructive values?
9. What kind of relationship did I have with my parents? Would I repeat the same mistakes my parents made or would I over-indulge or restrict my child in an attempt not to repeat my parents' mistakes?
10. How much would I worry about my child's health and safety? Would I be able to take care of a hurt or sick child?
11. What if my decision to have a child turns out to have been wrong for me?

What do I expect to gain from the parenting experience?

1. Do I enjoy child-centered activities?
2. Would having a child show others I am a mature person?
3. Would I want my child to be a miniature version of me? Would I be willing to adopt a child?
4. Would I feel comfortable if my child had ideas different from mine? How different?
5. Would I expect my child to make contributions I wish I had made in the world?
6. Would I expect my child to keep me from being lonely in my old age?
7. Would I be prepared emotionally to let my child leave when he/she grows up?
8. Would I expect my child to fulfill my relationship with my partner?
9. Do I need parenthood to fulfill my role as a man or woman?
10. Do I need a child to make my life meaningful?
11. Would I feel strongly about wanting my child to be a boy/girl? What if I didn't get the one I wanted?

Have I adequately discussed the parenting question with my partner

1. Does my partner want to have a child? Is he/she willing to ask these questions of himself/herself? Have we adequately discussed our reasons for wanting a child?
2. Do my partner and I understand each other's feelings about religion, work, family, child raising, future goals? Are our feelings compatible? Are they conducive to good parenting?
3. Would both my partner and I contribute our fair shares in raising the child?
4. Could we provide a child with a really good home environment? Is our relationship stable? Do we have a good sexual relationship?
5. After having a child, would my partner and I be able to separate if we should have unsolvable problems? Or would we feel obligated to remain together for the sake of the child?
6. Would we be able to share each other with a child without jealousy?
7. Do we want to bring a child into today's overpopulated world to face the social problems of our times?
8. Does my partner or do I have a hereditary abnormality we might pass on to a child? Could I emotionally and financially deal with having a physically or mentally handicapped child?
9. Suppose one of us wants a child and the other one doesn't. Who wins?
10. Which of the questions in this pamphlet do we really need to discuss before making a decision?

to parenting?

1. Would a child interfere with my educational plans? Would I have the energy to go to school and raise a child at the same time?
2. Would a child restrict my individual growth and development?
3. Could I handle children and a career well? Am I tired when I come home from work or do I have lots of energy left?
4. Does my job or my partner's job require a lot of traveling?
5. Am I financially able to support a child? Am I prepared to spend almost $100 a week to rear my child to age 18? or over $80,000, not including one partner's income loss if he/she would choose to remain at home?
6. Do I live in a neighborhood conducive to raising a child? Would I be willing to move?
7. Would I be willing to give up the freedom to do what I want to do, when I want to do it?
8. Would I be willing to restrict my social life? Would I miss lost leisure time and privacy?
9. Would my partner and I be prepared to spend more time at home? Would we have enough time to spend with a child?
10. Would I be willing to devote a great part of my life, at **least** 18 years, to being responsible for a child? and spend my entire life being concerned about my child's welfare?
11. Would I be prepared to be a single parent if my partner left or died?

Good luck in making your decision, and good wishes for a happy and fulfilled future.

This paper was prepared by Carole Goldman, Executive Director of the National Organization for Non-Parents, in cooperation with Elizabeth K. Canfield, Health and Family Planning Counselor, University of Southern California; Dr. Robert E. Gould, Professor of Psychiatry, New York Medical College; and Dr. Burleigh Seaver, Research Associate, Pennsylvania State University Institute for Research on Human Resources.

Additional copies of "AM I PARENT MATERIAL?" are available from the National Organization for Non-Parents, 806 Reisterstown Road, Baltimore, Md. 21208.
1-9, 6c each; 10-99, 5c each; 100 or more 4c each

PARENT MATERIAL?:

A thoughtful questionnaire about the most important decision I'll ever make.

These questions are posed to you as you consider the most important decision you will ever make—whether or not to have a child. The decision to have a child is one that you will live with for the rest of your life. The responsibility of a new life is awesome. These questions are designed to raise ideas that you may not have otherwise considered. There are no "right" answers and no "grades". You must decide for yourself what your answers reveal about your aptitude for parenthood.

You **do** have a choice. Exercise that choice with knowledge and careful thought. And then do what seems right for you.

Am I ready to raise a child?

1. Do I like children? Have I had enough experiences with babies? toddlers? teenagers?
2. Do I enjoy teaching others?
3. Do I communicate easily with others?
4. Do I have enough love to give a child? Can I express affection easily?
5. Would I have the patience to raise a child? Can I tolerate noise and confusion? Can I deal with disrupted schedules?
6. How do I handle anger? Would I abuse my child if I lost my temper?
7. What do I know about discipline and freedom? about setting limits and giving space? Would I be too strict? too lenient? Am I a perfectionist? How do I deal with change?
8. Do I know my own values and goals yet? Could I help my child develop constructive values?
9. What kind of relationship did I have with my parents? Would I repeat the same mistakes my parents made or would I over-indulge or restrict my child in an attempt not to repeat my parents' mistakes?
10. How much would I worry about my child's health and safety? Would I be able to take care of a hurt or sick child?
11. What if my decision to have a child turns out to have been wrong for me?

What do I expect to gain from the parenting experience?

1. Do I enjoy child-centered activities?
2. Would having a child show others I am a mature person?
3. Would I want my child to be a miniature version of me? Would I be willing to adopt a child?
4. Would I feel comfortable if my child had ideas different from mine? How different?
5. Would I expect my child to make contributions I wish I had made in the world?
6. Would I expect my child to keep me from being lonely in my old age?
7. Would I be prepared emotionally to let my child leave when he/she grows up?
8. Would I expect my child to fulfill my relationship with my partner?
9. Do I need parenthood to fulfill my role as a man or woman?
10. Do I need a child to make my life meaningful?
11. Would I feel strongly about wanting my child to be a boy/girl? What if I didn't get the one I wanted?

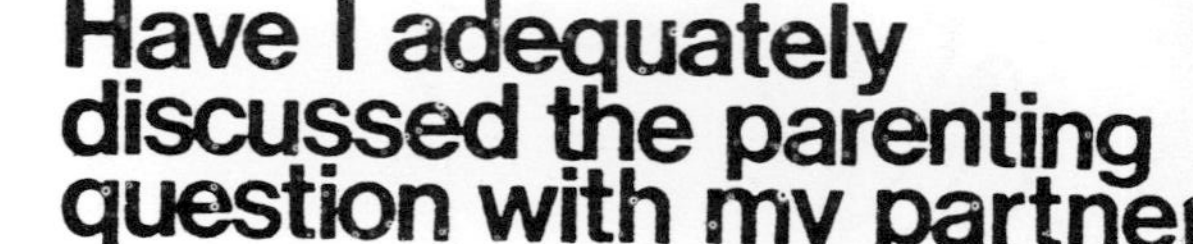

Have I adequately discussed the parenting question with my partner

1. Does my partner want to have a child? Is he/she willing to ask these questions of himself/herself? Have we adequately discussed our reasons for wanting a child?
2. Do my partner and I understand each other's feelings about religion, work, family, child raising, future goals? Are our feelings compatible? Are they conducive to good parenting?
3. Would both my partner and I contribute our fair shares in raising the child?
4. Could we provide a child with a really good home environment? Is our relationship stable? Do we have a good sexual relationship?
5. After having a child, would my partner and I be able to separate if we should have unsolvable problems? Or would we feel obligated to remain together for the sake of the child?
6. Would we be able to share each other with a child without jealousy?
7. Do we want to bring a child into today's overpopulated world to face the social problems of our times?
8. Does my partner or do I have a hereditary abnormality we might pass on to a child? Could I emotionally and financially deal with having a physically or mentally handicapped child?
9. Suppose one of us wants a child and the other one doesn't. Who wins?
10. Which of the questions in this pamphlet do we really need to discuss before making a decision?

THE EFFECTS OF BECOMING A PARENT AT DIFFERENT AGES*

	Teens	20's	30's	40's
Social Life:				
Income:				
Education:				
Career:				
Health:				
Life style:				

*Developed by Parent Education Project Staff, Iowa State University, 1979.

MY FEELINGS ABOUT BECOMING A PARENT*

(Rating Scale)

Directions: Circle your response and explain why you chose your response.

A = Agree U = Undecided D = Disagree

1. I can handle children and a job at the same time. A U D

2. I can afford to support a child. A U D

3. I would be willing to cut back on my social life and spend more time at home. A U D

4. I want to have a child to impress my friends. A U D

5. I think a child would make my life happy. A U D

6. I like to do things with children. A U D

7. I am willing to sacrifice my time, wants and privacy to take care of a child. A U D

8. I understand how children grow and develop. A U D

9. I am willing to give up my educational plans to have a child. A U D

10. I can go to school and take care of a child. A U D

11. I can share my love with my child and my spouse. A U D

12. I have had several experiences with babies, toddlers, and teenagers. A U D

---

*Developed by Parent Education Project Staff, Iowa State University, 1979.

FACTORS THAT INFLUENCE MY DECISION TO PARENT*

Directions: Check the column that best describes your reaction. Be prepared to discuss reasons for your responses.

	Yes	Undecided	No
1. My parents want grandchildren.			
2. I like children.			
3. I can afford to have a baby.			
4. I will be somebody if I have a child.			
5. I like to be needed.			
6. A baby will give me something to do.			
7. A baby could help a marriage.			
8. I want to prove that I am a woman and/or man.			
9. I don't want to be different.			
10. I want my child to have things I never had.			
11. I have always wanted a child.			
12. I enjoy contributing to the development of children.			

Note: The teacher may add more.

*Developed by Parent Education Project Staff, Iowa State University, 1979.

DECISIONS AND RESPONSIBILITIES*

SITUATION:

DECISIONS	CONSEQUENCES	REACTIONS	RESPONSIBILITIES

*Developed by Parent Education Project Staff, Iowa State University, 1979.

BIBLIOGRAPHY

Ames, B. Child Care and Development. Philadelphia: J. B. Lippincott Co., 1970.

Am I Parent Material? Baltimore, Maryland: National Alliance for Optional Parenthood.

Babcock, D., and Keepers, T. Raising Kids O.K. New York: Avon Publishers, 1976.

Baker, K. R., and Fane, X. Understanding and Guiding Young Children. Englewood Cliffs, N.J.: Prentice-Hall, 1976.

Bowman, H. A. Marriage for Moderns (7th ed.). New York: McGraw-Hill.

Brisbane, H., and Riker, A. The Developing Child. Peoria, Illinois: Charles A. Bennett Co., 1971.

Caplan, F. The Parenting Advisor. Garden City, N.Y.: Anchor Press/Doubleday, 1977.

Children's Rights. Chicago: National PTA.

Clark, L. The Cost and Value of American Children. Washington, D.C.: Population Reference Bureau, 1977.

Craig, F. Teenage Parenthood: A Web of Heartaches. Des Moines Sunday Register, November 12, 1978.

Craig, H. T. Thresholds to Adult Living. Peoria, Illinois: Charles A. Bennett Co., 1976.

Cross, A. Enjoying Family Living. Philadelphia: J. B. Lippincott Co., 1967.

David, L. I Refused to Give Up My Baby. Seventeen, June 1977, pp. 162-63, 183, 194.

Dinkmeyer, D., and McKay, G. Parents Handbook: Systematic Training for Effective Parenting. Circle Pines, Minn.: American Guidance Service, 1976.

Dodson, F. How to Father. Los Angeles: Nash Publications, 1974.

Dodson, F. How to Parent. New York: Signet Books, 1971.

Dolloff, P., and Resnik, M. Patterns of Life: Human Growth and Development. Columbus, Ohio: Merrill Publishing Co., 1972.

Draper, M., and Draper, H. Caring for Children. Peoria, Illinois: Charles A. Bennett Co., 1975.

Exploring Childhood. Cambridge, Mass.: Education Development Center, 1977.

Exter, M. A Time to Choose. Co-ed, Apr. 1978, pp. 68-70, 78.

Families in Stress. (DHEW Pub. No. OHDS-79030162). Washington, D.C.: U.S. Dept. of HEW.

Fisher, R. M. Eggs Help Teach Responsibility. Illinois Teacher, 1976, p. 139.

Fooner, A. Teen Marriage. Co-ed, Sept. 1977, pp. 77-106.

For Every Child. Des Moines, Iowa: Iowa Council for Children, 1978.

Forum. New York: J. C. Penney Co., Spring-Summer 1979.

Gelatt, H., Varenhorst, B., Carey, R., and Miller, G. Decisions and Outcomes. New York: College Entrance Examination Board, 1973.

Ginott, H. Between Parent and Child. New York: Macmillan, 1965.

Ginott, H. Between Parent and Teenager. New York: Avon Books, 1971.

Ginott, H. Driving Children Sane. New York: Macmillan, 1974.

Gordon, S., and Wollin, N. Parenting: A Guide for Young People. New York: William H. Sadlier, 1975.

Gordon, T. Parent Effectiveness Training. New York: Peter H. Wyden, 1970.

Hassles of Becoming a Teenage Parent. (DHEW Pub. No. HSA 78 5624). Washington, D.C.: U.S. Dept. of HEW.

Havighurst, R. Developmental Tasks and Education. New York: David McKay Co., 1976.

Healthy Babies: Chance or Choice?--A Workbook. White Plains, N.Y.: National Foundation--March of Dimes, 1979.

Hughes, H.M. Life in Families. Am. Sociological Assoc., 1970.

Hurlock, E. Child Growth and Development. New York: Webster Division, McGraw-Hill, 1978.

Inside Your Body, Inside Your Head. White Plains, N.Y.: National Foundation--March of Dimes, 1978.

Kloosterhouse, V. Trying On Parenthood. What's New in Home Economics, 1978, p. LP-2.

Landis, J. T., and Landis, M. G. Building a Successful Marriage (7th ed.). Englewood Cliffs, N.J.: Prentice Hall

Landis, J. T., and Landis, M. G. Personal Adjustment: Marriage and Family Living. Englewood Cliffs, N.J.: Prentice-Hall, 1970.

Levine, J. A. Who Will Raise the Children. Philadelphia: J. B. Lippincott Co., 1976.

Mama Spanks Me. Curriculum in Child Development and Family Relations. State of Iowa, 1956.

Marks, J. Don't Kid Yourself--Are You Ready for Parenthood? Teen Magazine, May 1979, p. 12+.

Norton, G. R. Parenting. Englewood Cliffs, N.J.: Prentice Hall, 1977.

Nye, F. I. School-Age Parenthood. Ames, Iowa: Iowa State University Cooperative Extension Service, 1978.

Paolucci, B., Faiola, T., and Thompson, P. Personal Perspectives. New York: McGraw-Hill, 1978.

Parenting in 1977: A Listing of Parenting Materials. Austin, Texas: Southwest Educational Development Laboratory, 1977.

Parenting Insights. Piscataway, N.J.: Johnson and Johnson, 1977.

Pinskey, D. Choosing Care for Your Child. Ames, Iowa: Iowa State University Cooperative Extension Service, 1977-78.

Porter, S. Sylvia Porter's Money Book. New York: Doubleday, 1975.

Right Now. McCalls, July 1978, pp. 45-52.

Ryder, V. Contemporary Living. South Holland, Ill.: The Goodheart-Willcox Co., 1979.

Sasse, C. Person to Person. Peoria, Ill.: Charles A. Bennett, 1978.

Satir, V. Peoplemaking. Palo Alto, California: Science and Behavior Books, 1972.

Simon, S. I Am Lovable and Capable. Niles, Ill.: Argus Communication, 1973.

Simon, S., Howe, L., Kirschenbaum, H. Values Clarification. New York: Hart Publishing, 1972.

Teenage Pregnancy. Co-ed, May 1978.

Wax, J. Teenage Pregnancy: Whose Fault? Seventeen, Oct. 1978, pp. 132, 172-73.

Westlake, H. G. Relationships A Study in Human Behavior. Lexington, Massachusetts: Ginn and Co., 1972.

Whelan, E. M. A Baby, Maybe? New York: Bobbs-Merrill Co., 1975.

Yamamata, K. The Child and His Image: Self-Concept in the Early Years. Boston: Houghton Mifflin Co., 1972.

RESOURCES

Films:

Forcing Children to Fail (Piaget)

He Acts His Age (McGraw-Hill)

Jamie, Story of a Sibling (McGraw-Hill)

Many Hear, Some Listen (Centron Films)

Personal Commitment, Where Do You Stand? (Guidance Associates)

Rock-A-Bye Baby (Psychology Today)

Sex Role Development (CRM Productions)

Teenage Father (March of Dimes)

War of the Eggs (Paulist Productions)

What Do You Mean and What Do I Mean? (Centron Films)

Woman-Child (March of Dimes)

You Can't Mean Not Ever? (University of Minnesota)

Filmstrips:

Decision-Making Skills . . . . Guidance Associates
757 Third Avenue
New York, N.Y. 10017

Children in Crises . . . . Parents' Magazine Films, Inc.
52 Vanderbilt Avenue
New York, N.Y. 10017
  Set #1, Child Abuse and Neglect

Conflicts Between Parents and Children
  Set #2, Parents Expect--Children Want

Mothers and Fathers
  Set #2, Family Relationships
  Set #3, Mother/Father Roles

The Economics of Parenthood
  Set #1, Laying the Groundwork

Understanding Early Childhood
  Set #1, The Child's Relationship with the Family

Understanding Parenthood
  Set #2, The Growing Parent

What Do I See When I See Me?
  Set #3, I See Strength

Preparation for Parenthood . . . . Sunburst Communications
Room 62
41 Washington Avenue
Pleasantville, N.Y. 10570

Reexamining Sex Roles: Evolution or Revolution?

Kits:

Parenting: Fathers, Mothers, and Others (J. C. Penney Co.)

Transparencies:

Rational Decision Making (3-M Transparencies)

Pamphlets:

Read to Your Child . . . . Positive Parent/Early Childhood Program, Southwest Educational Development Laboratory, 211 East 7th Street, Austin, Texas 78701

Praise Your Children

Pay Attention to Young Children

Miscellaneous Addresses:

National Alliance for Optional Parenthood
3 North Liberty Street
Baltimore, Maryland 21201

National Parent Teachers Association
700 N. Rust Street
Chicago, Illinois 60611

Iowa Council for Children
523 East 12th Street
Des Moines, Iowa 50319

National Foundation--March of Dimes
Box 2000
White Plains, New York 10602

Write for:

Catalog - Public Health Education Materials on Birth Defects and Prenatal Care.

Superintendent of Documents
U.S. Government Printing Office (for DHEW publications)
Washington, D.C. 20402

Johnson and Johnson
Consumer and Professional Services
Piscataway, New Jersey 08854

Population Reference Bureau, Inc.
1337 Connecticut Avenue, N.W.
Washington, D.C. 20036